Inner
Compass

Inner Compass

An Invitation to Ignatian Spirituality

MARGARET SILF

an imprint of
Loyola Press

Chicago

an imprint of

Loyola Press
3441 North Ashland Avenue
Chicago, Illinois 60657

Published in Great Britain by Darton, Longman & Todd, Ltd. as
Landmarks: An Ignatian Journey, © 1998 Margaret Silf

All quotations from Scripture are from the Jerusalem Bible © by
Darton, Longman & Todd, Ltd., and Doubleday, a division of
Bantam Doubleday Dell, Inc. Reprinted by permission.

Interior design by Amy Evans McClure

Library of Congress Cataloging-in-Publication Data
Silf, Margaret.
    Inner Compass: an invitation to ignatian spirituality / by Margaret Silf
        p.   cm.
    Rev. ed. of: Landmarks. London, Darton, Longman & Todd ©1998
    ISBN 0-8294-1366-9 (pbk.)
    1.Igantius, of Loyola, Saint 1491–1556   Exercitia spiritualia.
        2. Spiritual Exercises.   I. Silf, Margaret Landmarks.   II. Title.
BX2179.L8S49   1999
248.3—dc21   99-22914
                                                            CIP

Printed in Canada

06 07 / 10 9 8 7 6

CONTENTS

Foreword

I KNOW OF NO PUBLISHING house that has ever offered to reimburse a buyer who remains dissatisfied after reading one of its books. I think Loyola Press could safely make the first such offer with *Inner Compass*.

If asked, "What is the subject that interests you most, and on which subject do you consider yourself most ignorant?" the true answer for all of us is "Me." If any readers recoil from this answer, they might ask themselves, "Do my ears prick up if I pass a group of people and hear them mention my name?" "Have I ever felt anxiety while awaiting the results of an examination, whether academic, medical, or vocational?" "When looking at photographs, some of which include me, do I give equal attention to every photograph?" "Do I spend as much time looking at other people as I spend looking at myself in a mirror?" "Why this disproportionate interest in me if I really know myself?"

Inner Compass looks at the most fundamental questions that concern every human being, whatever their race, culture, religion, or state in life. "Where are you?" "How are you and why?" "Who are you?" These fundamental questions were explored by St. Ignatius Loyola, a sixteenth-century Basque, in his book the *Spiritual Exercises,* which offers methods of discovering for oneself the answer to these basic questions. A friend of Ignatius, Jerome Nadal, on being asked for whom the *Spiritual*

Exercises were suited, answered, "For Catholics, for Protestants, and for pagans"! *Inner Compass* is similarly suited.

I am very familiar with the *Spiritual Exercises*. Overfamiliarity has not bred contempt, but it does tend to breed boredom with books on Ignatian spirituality. In reading *Inner Compass,* I was never bored for a moment, but delighted in following Margaret Silf's journey of exploration today, using the landmarks that Ignatius offered four hundred years ago. They are landmarks, not pillars supporting an immovable shelter in which all readers must find refuge. The book encourages further exploration and provides a variety of exercises at the end of each chapter so that readers can make discoveries for themselves.

Inner Compass is lucidly written, down-to-earth, free of jargon, and full of hope and encouragement. Ignatius wrote his *Exercises* as a way of helping us to see and find the will of God. Finding the will of God can sometimes feel, in the author's words, "like playing darts on an invisible board." In this book she helps us to find the will of God within our own hearts, a will that is never directed to only our individual benefit, but always to the well-being of all peoples and of all creation.

Gerard W. Hughes
December 1997

Preface @

THE SALAD BOWL

NOT LONG AGO, I was invited to attend a friend's induction as vicar of his new parish. After the service, his new parishioners had put on a marvelous feast in the church hall. The trestle tables were set out with all kinds of goodies. The congregation streamed out of the church and into the hall. The place became alive with conversation, and, as so often happens at these gatherings, within ten minutes the laden tables were almost bare . . . except for one large bowl of rice salad, which remained untouched in the middle of a long, empty table. I happened to notice this salad, and my heart went out to the person who had brought it as a love-offering. How hurt and saddened that person must be feeling, I thought. And my second thought was, "Why has nobody eaten it? It looks so appetizing and inviting!"

Then it became obvious why the salad stood deserted and untouched after the feast was over. There was no spoon. The fact hit me like a sledgehammer that night. I realized that the salad bowl was telling me something about the Church. It, too, is sometimes like a bowl of salad, full of what people are so longing to receive, so hungry for. But where is the spoon? Shall the treasure remain forever on display, the inaccessible centerpiece of an empty table? Do God's people really have the means to eat the food he prepares for them, or is it wrapped in the cellophane of doctrine and set high on the top shelf of theology? And are they too well trained to dare to mention the problem?

No one can know the mind of God. Yet surely he, like us, is saddened and grieved when his hungry children stand empty-handed at
his table because "the Church" has provided no spoons for the salad.
Let us not complain; let us rather remember that we are the Church, and
that it is up to us, his people, to make the feast accessible to all, in whatever ways open up to us.

I can add nothing to the salad. I venture only to offer a little spoon.
And I can do that only because others have been "spoons" for me in my
own hunger for the living bread. They have made it possible for me to
share in the feast. I would like to thank them for this quiet ministry that
they may not even have realized they were engaged in. . . .

I thank my cousin, Ralph Wells, who influenced my childhood more
than he or I quite realized, by his steady, unshakable, uncompromising
faith. I thank Michael Paton, who accompanied my adolescent awakening to a deepening of faith as he prepared me for confirmation, and
Madeleine, my friend who died at that time, aged fifteen, already a candle for God that time hasn't extinguished in my heart. And I thank my
parents, Irene and Bernard Ashton, who gave me the gift of growing up
in a home where there was love.

I thank Brian McClorry, who carried me home when I had wandered
far from my own truth, and has remained my patient, gentle, and challenging companion through the years that are leading from truth to freedom. I thank Gerry Hughes for walking with me through the journey of
the *Exercises* and beyond, for his wisdom in words and his communion
in silence, and for the sheer gift of his presence. I especially thank Brian
and Gerry for all their help and encouragement during the evolution of
this book, and for their tremendous support and facilitation of the ministry of lay spiritual companionship that they have done so much, personally, to bring about.

I thank my husband, Klaus, for his support and encouragement as
a fellow traveler, for his untiring energy in making possible the quiet
days for which this material was written, and for his invaluable techni-
cal expertise when it comes to using computers and other mysterious
machinery. And I thank my daughter, Kirstin, for keeping my heart in
heaven and my feet firmly on the earth.

I thank Terry Biddington for drawing me, against my own reluctance, into the first (to my knowledge) Ignatian discovery group in North Staffordshire, and for guiding me into the ways of imaginative prayer.

So many people have shared their own inner treasure with me and have thereby enriched me more than they can imagine. Most especially, I would like to thank my friends in the Christian communities in the Keele University Chaplaincy and in Norton-le-Moors, Stoke-on-Trent, for whom this material was originally written.

Almost all of the examples in the book are drawn from my own personal prayer. I would, however, like to acknowledge a debt of gratitude particularly to Elizabeth McNulty, who opened up for me, and for many others, the insights on the nature of Sabbath time in chapter 1 and to Gerald O'Mahony, who demonstrated so vividly the effects of "facing the sun" in chapter 4.

Since it was first written, *Inner Compass* has sailed the Atlantic. I would like to say a special thank-you to Loyola Press's LaVonne Neff, Linda Schlafer, and Rita George, who have done so much to make this transition an enjoyable adventure.

Finally, my thanks go to all who have walked alongside me in retreats and at other significant times in my life and have opened my eyes to the possibility of "living the *Exercises*," especially Helen Bamber, Renate Düllmann, Teresa Foster, the late Arnold Freeman, the late Paul Glendinning, Damian Jackson, John Marbaix, Tom McGuinness, the late Donald Nicholl, Tom Shufflebottom, and supremely, Brian and Gerry. I thank you from my heart.

Before You Begin

THIS BOOK IS A COMPANION for your inner journey. Take it gently, and enjoy the landscape as you go. Don't rush at it like a fell runner, intent on breaking the land speed record. The more you savor the journey, the more you will benefit from it.

Some people like to take their walks alone. If you are journeying alone with this book, take the walk in your own good time, stopping wherever you feel the urge to do so. Feel the bark of the trees, dip your fingers in the stream, gaze at the sunset for as long as you wish. It will probably be unhelpful to try to journey through more than one chapter at a time, and you may find that it suits you better just to explore one small section. Pick and choose from the suggested exercises at the end of each chapter. Stay with any that appeal to you and leave alone those that don't. You can safely trust your own sense of inner resonance to show you what is for you and what is not. You may find that the material in the book can offer you spiritual companionship through a sustained, home-based prayer journey or retreat within the context of your daily life.

Solitary travelers can, however, become lonely and disheartened and can sometimes lose their bearings. You might find it very helpful to find a companion with whom you can share your experience from time to time — a trusted friend who is on your wavelength, perhaps, or even someone you do not yet know personally but who is willing to walk alongside you as, together, you seek to discern where God is for you on your inner journey. To find a "soul-friend" may seem a daunting task: my advice is to look around your own circle of friends and fellow believers to notice any among them who are clearly people of prayer themselves (it usually shows, if you are observant, and it may not be the people you would expect). Approach such a person and explain very simply what you are looking for. They may be very happy to walk beside you themselves or to recommend someone else who could be the right companion for you.

Other people prefer to journey in groups. If you are using the book as the basis for a faith-sharing group, you will find that each chapter will give you material for the equivalent of one full day of reflection, with time to follow up some of the suggested exercises in a prayerful atmosphere. Optionally, you might share your reactions and responses with other members of the group. This sharing of experiences between trusted friends is perhaps the most valuable exercise of all. The facilitator should ensure that everyone in the group has an opportunity to share to the extent that they wish to do so (no coercion, please). And it goes without saying that complete confidentiality within the group is an absolute must: this requirement needs to be made clear from the outset.

When sharing spiritual experience like this, simply allow each person to contribute, leaving a respectful few moments' silence between one speaker and the next. There should be no interruption or discussion (since this is a journey of the heart, not an exercise of the head), and no attempt to "correct" anyone's views or to offer advice. The truth that underpins this kind of faith sharing is that each person's experience is wholly and unquestionably valid and is offered as a gift of trust to the others. The aim should be that all come away from the encounter with increased confidence in their own experience and a deepened sense of their own unique value before God and to their peers. Remember that when we open our heart's experience to each other in trust, we are entering on holy ground, where there is no place for comment, criticism, or correction, but only for a response of loving acceptance. On this holy ground, God-in-you is listening to God-in-the-other.

If you are using the material for shorter faith-sharing meetings, you may prefer to use just one or two sections at a time. The chapters have subdivisions, each with its own heading, to give you a guide. It will be helpful if participants have an opportunity to read the material for themselves in advance of the group meeting, and perhaps to use it as a focus for personal prayer. The group leader should, ideally, be familiar with the whole book and have a sense of its shape and purpose before beginning the program. The suggested exercises can then be evaluated in light of the needs of individual group members. One model is for a facilitator to summarize the material at each meeting and then let participants use it for personal reflection over the subsequent week, so they can share their reflections at the start of the next meeting.

It is important that the material be used in the order given, since it follows the dynamic of the *Spiritual Exercises* and each chapter builds on the reader's familiarity with what has gone before. However, it is not a commentary on the *Spiritual Exercises,* much less a way of actually making the *Exercises*. Having said that, a number of the participants in two pilot programs have gone on to make the full *Exercises* in daily life, under personal direction, and have found *Inner Compass* to be a valuable preparation for this encounter. A national and international network of Ignatian faith-sharing groups and Christian Life Communities exists to help people who wish to take their journey further in this particular way. Contact addresses are given below, if you would like more information.

You may like to structure your meetings around shared prayer, possibly with appropriate music. A few sources that we have found helpful in the pilot programs are mentioned below; you will, of course, want to add your own choices. A few helpful book titles are also suggested as recommended further reading.

If at all possible, encourage your group to be ecumenical. You will quickly discover, if you haven't already done so, that when people begin to share the deeper reaches of their hearts' journeys, the denominational divisions fall away without any compromise of the genuine variety of riches between different traditions. The truth unites, and this is a journey toward truth. You will discover this most fully if your group is nondenominational and open to people who are not aligned to any established church tradition at all.

How many people make a group? Where there are two or three gathered, there is a group, and there is God among them. At the other end of the scale, you may find that if numbers go above twenty, it would be wise to split into two or more smaller groups. If intimate faith sharing is central to your meetings, a maximum number of about six is more appropriate.

And where to meet? Do try to find a congenial space. Often it is good to meet in each other's homes when the group size permits. Church halls and school classrooms are not comfortable on the whole, and tend to be loaded with denominational bias or negative memories. In Stoke-on-Trent we have been very fortunate in enjoying the hospitality of the local Franciscan community for one of the groups, and we have met in our own homes with the other. You may find that a local religious community would welcome your approaches.

Finally, on the practical side, do keep costs to an absolute minimum. The whole ethos of daily life faith sharing and spiritual journeying is that it should be freely accessible, especially to those people who lack the time, the money, or the freedom of circumstances to make formal retreats. Freely you have received; give as freely as you can. Quiet days, or simply quiet hours, can be arranged in each other's homes at no more cost than a pot of tea or coffee. Encourage everyone to bring a contribution for a potluck lunch or supper, and you will be surprised at what interesting meals come together. If you use other premises or invite outside speakers, simply ask each participant for a small contribution toward a donation to your hosts or to reimburse your guests' traveling expenses.

The two original (ecumenical) pilot groups still meet regularly to share their journeys and to become a resource for others. They join me in praying for every blessing upon your journey.

Music for the Journey

Dana: "The Gift of Love"; "In the Palm of His Hand"
Bernadette Farrell: "Christ Be Our Life"; "God Beyond All Names"

Carey Landry: "Abba, Father"; "I Will Not Forget You," vols.1 and 2
Tom McGuinness: "Winter Gifting"; "Exultet"; "All Will Be Well"
Marilla Ness: "He Touched Me"; "Come Back to Me"; "Heart of Love"; "Abba My Father"
St. Louis Jesuits: "Earthen Vessels"
General/Instrumental: For example, "Praise Him on the Pan Pipes" (Simon Bernard-Smith); "Angel Voices," "Songs of Zion" (Maurice Sklar); "Songs of Taize" (Kingsway); "Soften My Heart" (Nick Fletcher; Classical Praise series)

Suggestions for Further Reading

William Barry, *God and You* (Paulist Press, 1988); *What Do I Want in Prayer?* (Paulist Press, 1994)
Charles Elliott, *Praying the Kingdom* (Darton, Longman & Todd, 1985)
Thomas H. Green, *Opening to God* (Walker Publishing Company, 1986)
Margaret Hebblethwaite, *Finding God in All Things* (Fount, 1994); *Six New Gospels* (Cowley, 1994)
Gerard W. Hughes, *God of Surprises* (Cowley, 1993); *God, Where Are You?* (Darton, Longman and Todd, 1997); *Oh God, Why?* (BRF, 1992)
William Johnston, *Being In Love* (Fount, 1989)
David Lonsdale, *Eyes to See, Ears to Hear* (Loyola Press, 1991)
Anthony de Mello, *Sadhana: A Way to God* (Doubleday & Company, 1984); *Awareness* (Doubleday & Company, 1992)
Donald Nicholl, *Holiness* (Darton, Longman & Todd, 1992)
Philip Sheldrake, *Befriending Our Desires* (Ave Maria Press, 1994)
Jean Vanier, *Our Journey Home* (Orbis Books, 1997)

TO MAKE CONTACT with an Ignatian network in your area:
Jesuit Conference
1616 P Street, NW
Suite 400
Washington, DC 20036-1405
Phone: 202-462-0400
Fax: 202-328-9212
E-mail: usjc@jesuit.org

TO MAKE CONTACT with a local Christian Life Community (faith-sharing group):

Christian Life Community
3601 Lindell Blvd.
St. Louis, MO 63108-3393
Phone: 314-977-7370
Web page: http://www.clc-usa.org/

MEET THE GUIDE

IN MY DAY JOB, I am writing a programmer's guide on how to overcome the problems in computer date management when we enter the next millennium. How come, then, I am sitting here reflecting on the ways in which the insights of a man who lived 450 years ago in a remote Basque village in northern Spain affect the way in which we relate to God today, on the threshold of the twenty-first century? I sometimes think that my PC will give a little shudder of culture shock when I expect it to process my thoughts on the problems of two-digit date notation and the search for my deepest desire at the same time.

This coming together of two worlds apparently so far removed from each other is perhaps in itself a pointer to some of the treasures that are ours today through the legacy of Ignatius Loyola and the Society of Jesus, which he founded. If we can imagine his browsing through this book, or sitting among us as we explore these questions together, he would quite likely be smiling to himself and muttering something about "finding God in all things." He would find it completely normal and healthy that we should be searching to deepen our relationship with God in the midst of life as we really live it—up to our ears in work or lack of it, mortgages, children, and mess. He would be delighted to find that most of us are laypeople, as he was when he was making his own journey of discovery. He would surely welcome the fact that we come from many different church traditions or even from none at all. And he would be more than tolerant of the checkered histories we may have behind us, remembering the excesses of his own misspent youth. Most of all, he would recognize the love of God that is burning inside each of us, that is always leading us onward, like a beacon, toward deepening our relationship with him, because this would reflect the experience of Ignatius's own heart and the source of his prodigious energy.

So who was this man whose life and discoveries are still affecting our own journeys so fruitfully? Before we begin our journey proper, let's indulge for a few minutes in a time shift that takes us back to the age when Europe was in a similar kind of between-age turmoil to the one we are experiencing now. This new age isn't just causing havoc to our computer systems but also seems to include a heightened awareness in people everywhere (whether they call themselves religious or not) that there is more to life than the mere management of our days to achieve comfort and security in the shifting landscapes of our lives.

Iñigo Lopez lived at the time when the world was coming painfully and violently out of the Middle Ages. The mere facts of his life can be summed up in a few sentences; its content was to be infinitely more far-reaching. He was born in 1491, the youngest of a family of thirteen, in Loyola, in the Basque region of northern Spain. When he was fourteen, he was sent away to train as a royal page to the king of Spain and was introduced to the ideals of chivalry and knightly service. As he grew older, he developed more than a passing interest in women, both those far away in his daydreams, and those who were temptingly accessible. The last thing on his mind during these years was his spiritual journey or the inner movements of his heart.

His life swerved around a big bend during his mid-twenties. The favor that his employer, Don Juan Velasquez, had enjoyed in the royal court came to an abrupt end at the death of the king. As a result, Iñigo himself was unemployed, and chastened by his experience of how quickly and easily the power of riches and influence can disappear. With a parting gift of a few hundred crowns and two horses from the widow of his former employer, he had to set off into the unknown and start again.

The next phase of his life was in the household of the duke of Najera, who employed him as a gentleman-at-arms. Iñigo learned to use weapons and helped to put down rebellions. His military training under the duke brought him, four years later, to a place called Pamplona, where he commanded a company defending the fortress there against a French invasion. The defense had become futile and defeat was a certainty, but Iñigo was stubborn to the limits and absolutely refused to surrender. The price of his resistance came in the form of a cannonball, which shattered his leg and broke his right knee. His days as a soldier ended on a stretcher; he was transported in agony and humiliation across the mountains to his family home in Loyola.

It must have seemed like the end of the line. Probably most of us can identify with that drained, empty feeling of being at the end of our dreams and our resources, or helpless in pain or immobility, either in body or in mind. We can imagine how it might have been for this young man, in the prime of his life, to lie a helpless invalid, wracked by pain, with nothing but his broken dreams for company. So daydreaming is just what he did.

Having asked in vain for some lively romantic novels to read, Iñigo had to make do with what the castle could offer, which turned out to be a *Life of Christ* and a *Lives of the Saints*. This stricken and disgruntled patient spent his time between reading and daydreaming of all that might have been, had his injury not robbed him, in a stroke, of both his future as a soldier and his attractiveness to women.

Daydreaming! Ironic that this man whose military skills and leadership potential were so remarkable should have come down to us, most powerfully, as a daydreamer. But Iñigo's daydreams held a potent secret. They had, locked up inside them, the key to the gift of discernment. And how did Iñigo discover for himself this key that was to open up a gold mine in his heart?

As the tedious, pain-ridden days passed, Iñigo indulged in two kinds of dreaming. On the one hand, he still dreamed of the battles he would command, the military glories he would achieve, the noble ladies he would woo and win. But they were the dreams of "what might have been," and though they raised his spirits for a short while as he enjoyed the fantasy, they left him, in the longer term, feeling flat and disconsolate.

On the other hand, fired by the books he had been given, he started to dream of a King whose service was potentially even more desirable than that of the king of Spain; he began to wonder how this Christ King might be served; he began to dream of outsainting the saints in this great new quest that might be worth spending his life on. They were still daydreams, but he noticed an important difference in their aftereffects. These dreams left him feeling inspired, energized, and eager. They were not about what might have been but about something that still lay dormant in the depths of his own heart, like a seed that had been mysteriously germinated and was pushing its way to the surface of his life through all this heavy soil of pain and disappointment. These were dreams that didn't go away.

It was into this realization of the difference between daydreams and God dreams (as we might call them) that the gift of discernment was given to Iñigo. It was there that he discovered what we might call the "inner compass" of his heart, which was able to reveal to him which movements within him were capable of engaging his deepest vital energy, and which were leading him only to fleeting satisfactions that left him unchanged and unfulfilled. As he lay there in his enforced stillness and solitude, he learned to notice his moods and feelings and reactions and to measure them against this unseen compass. In his inner silence, he listened with fresh awareness to an invitation coming from deep inside himself to enlist in the adventure of the service of God.

As he ventured more and more deeply into the stories that were inspiring his new kind of daydreaming, he was also finding a new way of exercising his imagination. He began to find himself, in imagination, present in the scenes, conversations, and stories of the Gospels, and he began to participate in the plots of these stories. It was the start, for him, of an adventure into imaginative prayer that was to become a most powerful catalyst for the growth of his personal relationship with God, a method of prayer that is just as vividly available to us today.

On his sickbed, Iñigo experienced deep conversion. Gradually, after many setbacks, he limped his way back to life, but it was never again to be the life that he had known before; the cannonball had blown that life to pieces. Now Iñigo was a pilgrim of God, to whom he was ready to offer all his ideals of knightly service, courage, and persistence. The next step was to tell his family . . . and, as for so many who have walked this path in their own personal ways since then (including, surely, many of you who are reading this book today), this wasn't easy! Against a backdrop of pressure to use his skills and gifts to bring honor to the family name and help maintain the family property, Iñigo made his excuses and left, with neither he nor his family knowing with any certainty where he was headed. Iñigo—the nobleman, the soldier, the fearless defender of Pamplona—had become Iñigo the pilgrim.

The first stage of the pilgrimage—that search for the "I know not what" that was urging him onwards—took Iñigo to the Abbey of Montserrat, high on a jagged mountain peak overlooking the plain of Manresa. Here he desired to make a full confession of the sins of his earlier life and begin again. His confession is said to have taken three days to make, and he received absolution from one of the monks there. He exchanged his nobleman's dress for the simple outfit of a poor pilgrim and made a night vigil of prayer. He gave his clothes to a beggar and his mule to the monks. He left his sword and dagger behind as an offering at the altar and as a sign that he had exchanged his life in the service of the world's values for one committed to the service of God.

As the new pilgrim made his way down the hill of Montserrat to the plain below, his mind must have been full of the experience of his conversion, his confession, his vigil, and the advice he had been given by the monks on the life of prayer. To all this new experience, he surely applied the ways of discernment that he had discovered in his dreams at Loyola. He felt the need to stay awhile, in quiet, to reflect on all that had passed and everything that God seemed to be showing him through it. He also made some notes on his reflections. And so it happened that, instead of going straight to Barcelona as he had intended, he settled in the nearby town of Manresa for "a few days," which stretched into eleven months. In Manresa, the next stage of his life took shape.

Determined to live true to all that he had promised God in Montserrat, the proud and self-willed Iñigo now faced a life of begging for his daily food, while submitting to the relentless mockery of street urchins who were probably better dressed and cared for than he was. Living out the high dream of the mountain when he was down on the plain in the heat and dust of everyday reality proved to be, for him as for us, a constant struggle. He treated himself harshly, but he never forgot the agony of his own long sickness at Loyola, and he turned that memory into service by trying to help the sick in the hospitals of Manresa. He prayed until prayer became part of his every waking moment. At last he found a cave near the river where he made himself a desert home. That cave was to become a space where his love and understanding of God would deepen beyond anything he could have imagined, where he would receive insights that remain fresh and valid for us today, and where, very important for us, he was to capture the fruits of his conversion, his prayer, and his reflections in written form.

Perhaps inevitably, given what a good thing was gestating in his heart, Iñigo also fell victim to the onslaught of negative movements, or "false spirits," as he would have called them. He suffered endless self-recrimination about his sins, real and imagined. He experienced dark depths of despair and came close to taking his own life. It was, perhaps, a black time, shot through with golden streaks of insight and passionate commitment to God, or it was a golden time of spiritual growth and maturing, shot through with the darkest shafts of doubt and despair. Either way of looking at it may find its parallels in our own experience—we have those times in our lives that are at once fraught with struggle and alight with the flame of our hearts' desires.

From Manresa came a man who had freely bound himself in joyful service to a king called Christ. He had been so opened to the inpouring of the Holy Spirit that he was able to interpret his own experience in a way that has universal validity and significance. The fruit of this experience and the wisdom that it engendered is recorded in an unassuming little book called the *Spiritual Exercises*. Iñigo's notebook was to become a guide, based entirely on his own experience, on how to become increasingly sensitive to God's action in our lives, how to discover and live true to the very deepest desires within us, how to make decisions that reflect God's indwelling presence in the innermost freedom of our

The Spiritual Exercises

• Discovering who I really am
• Directing myself toward God
• Noticing God's action in my life
• Responding to the movements of my heart
• Discovering the nature of my deepest desire
• Seeking God's will
• Becoming free of all that distracts me from my deepest desire
• Making choices in line with my truest self
• Connecting my lived experience with the life, death, and resurrection of Christ
• Responding to God's love for me
• Finding God in all things

hearts, and how to join our lives consciously with the life of Jesus, God-made-man, through the living spirit of the gospel.

It would be nice to record that Iñigo went from strength to strength in his life of discipleship. Of course, it wasn't so. How could it be? We all know, too well, that things are never like that. Iñigo's dream of serving God in the Holy Land was intractably vetoed by the authorities there. His travels were overtaken by ill health and near shipwreck. His attempts to help others by sharing his *Exercises* in spiritual conversations brought opposition from the Church, which eventually subjected him to the Inquisition, and the secular authorities, who among other things threatened him with a public birching. Injustice, humiliation, and betrayal became his familiar companions, but they were carrying a hidden gift: through them he came to realize that his desire to be with Christ was stronger than his desire to avoid the indignities and disgraces that the world and the Church meted out to him.

Despite all this, the word *companion* became central to Iñigo's life. In Manresa, Iñigo had already begun to share his experiences with a few friends who showed interest in his *Exercises*. He used his own notes as a guide to helping them. This continues to be the way in which the *Exercises* are used: as a guide to a director, mentor, or soul-friend in helping another person discover, through prayer and reflection, God's action in his or her life.

Iñigo's ministry of companionship grew stronger when he became a student in Paris, belatedly trying to acquire the academic qualifications that would overcome the objections the Church raised against his speaking to others of spiritual matters without ecclesiastical authority. He was eventually ordained in 1536 at the age of forty-five and adopted the name Ignatius. Before this, though, he and his friends in Paris, Francis

Xavier and Peter Favre, were to deepen their friendship into a bond that forged them into the first Jesuits, as together they formed the Society of Jesus. By 1534, this little group of companions had grown to seven, and on August 15 of that year they bound themselves into an embryonic religious order. On that day they shared the Eucharist together, made their vows, and then celebrated . . . with a picnic!

Over 450 years separate us from that inconspicuous event on the outskirts of Paris. For the first seven Jesuits, there was surely no sense of disconnection between the deep seriousness of their commitment to God and to each other and the simple, exuberant joy of their celebratory picnic. Among the many riches that have come down to us from that small group of friends, we might focus on that coming together of all that makes us human: our searching and desiring, our failing and falling and fun loving, our shipwrecks and our picnics.

Just as my computer accepts all that comes, whether it be ancient spiritualities or problems of binary notation, so our inner journeys, surely, are about all of us, just as we are, with no arbitrary demarcations between work and prayer, between secular and spiritual, or between God and "real life." Ignatian spirituality is about finding God in our lived experience and allowing him to transform that experience, through his Spirit, for ourselves and for the whole human family.

The explorations in this book, like Ignatius's own, also began as a response to groups of friends who wanted to come together to share their search for God. Like his, they are carved out of personal experience—some of it joyful, some of it painful, all of it lived. They are offered in the spirit of Ignatius in the hope that they may provide a few landmarks in the mysterious and sometimes hazardous terrain of our hearts, as we make the journey inward toward the pearl of great price that lies both at our own deepest center and far beyond our wildest imaginings.

On a journey we use landmarks to give us a point of recognition. We notice something we recognize—some feature of the landscape—and it locates our position: "Yes, I recognize that! So I must be somewhere around there." They give us confidence that we are not completely lost. They help us to find our bearings and discern the direction for the next stage of the journey. When we are in unfamiliar terrain (and life, for all of us, as we move into the future, is unfamiliar terrain), landmarks help us to locate ourselves and encourage us to keep walking. Something outside ourselves—something that everyone can see and recognize (even though they may see it from a different perspective and give it a different name) relates to precisely where we are. It places us, as individuals, within the wider landscape.

Maps and guidebooks would do just as well, you might say. And when it comes to the spiritual journey of our hearts, there is no shortage of maps and guidebooks, ranging from the "Go this way, or else!" variety of creed and catechism, to the "Fifty ways to climb the ladder of perfection" sort. The thing they all have in common is that they can be read in an armchair. They can all teach you how to swim without getting wet.

Landmarks won't let you do that. They are of no use at all unless you are on the road! They are effective only in that they connect where you are, in your own lived experience, to a point of recognition and orientation, for your own story and for the whole human story.

I remember once smiling over a particularly colorful description of a walk by the late A. Wainwright in one of his mountain walk guides, which included the bizarre instruction to "turn left at the third hawthorn tree." This unlikely piece of wisdom made a gentle mockery of all the intricately drawn maps in the book. That third hawthorn tree just had to be discovered. It was a clue on a treasure hunt, and it demanded not only that I actually make the walk but that I do it *now*, before the number and arrangement of the hawthorn trees should change beyond recognition. It was information distilled from his own walking of the path, and gladly, exuberantly, shared with me, his reader and fellow walker. The excitement of his own discovery infected me with the desire to make my own. It felt both personal and universal, rich with the paradox of a season ticket valid only for the present moment.

Landmarks, like hawthorn trees, are also useful only when there is some light to see by. Even people who are on the way and committed to following the right path will encounter times of obscurity and darkness when the evidence is hidden or the signals are mixed. *Inner Compass* also explores ways of developing the skills and resources needed for those times when we walk by faith and not by sight.

Perhaps the landmarks in this book share something of the quality of Wainwright's third hawthorn tree. You may recognize them, though you might not call them by the names I know them by. I hope they may help you find your own way to the greater treasure beyond the clues and encourage you to use your own inner compass with confidence and trust. But you won't find them until you take the risk of losing yourself, by setting out and by keeping going, in the timeless urgency of the present moment. This kind of journey is not for "pillars of the Church." It is for "people of the way."

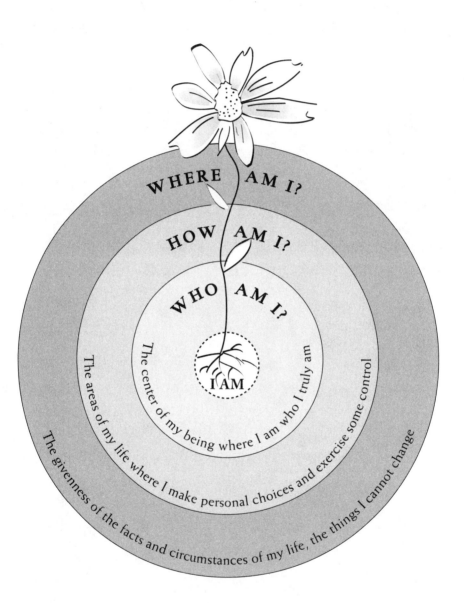

WHERE AM I?

HOW AM I?

WHO AM I?

The center of my being where I am who I truly am

I AM

The areas of my life where I make personal choices and exercise some control

The givenness of the facts and circumstances of my life, the things I cannot change

1

WHERE AM I? HOW AM I?
WHO AM I?

B EFORE WE BEGIN to explore the particular ways in which Ignatian
spirituality can help our inner journey, we need to take a look at our
inner landscape, to establish our bearings and see where we actually are.
That is the purpose of this first chapter, and to help in this locating exercise, I ask you to imagine three concentric circles.

We might call the outermost ring the *Where* circle. Its perimeter represents all those things in my life that I cannot change: my natural family, my genetic makeup, the place and culture into which I was born, my
upbringing, my education, all the things that have already happened to
me, my natural giftedness and my inborn shortcomings, my health and
my disabilities. These things form the givenness of my life; they are the
facts of my existence. They are, quite simply, where I am. Not only can
I do nothing to change them, but they occupy almost all of my consciousness and my energy. Whether I like it or not, I live here, on the
outside edge of myself, for most of my waking hours.

Now let's move inward to the second circle. I call this my *How* circle, because it is the area of my life where I can exercise some choice.
Here things happen to me, but I can choose how to respond to them.
I can accept or reject, condone or confront, go with the flow or stand
up to be counted. I can make personal relationships and take personal

initiatives. Every minute that I live changes the kaleidoscope of events that bombard me, and every choice I make subtly but certainly goes toward making me how I am. Choices turn into habits, and habits become character. And this process goes further than the boundaries of myself. My choices, my habits, and my character make subtle but certain changes to the "how" of the whole human family. My choices for truth make the world more truthful. My betrayals of my own integrity undermine the integrity of all.

For many people the journey stops here. They live in a world where events happen to them, and they make choices about how to react to those events. A few take the risk of going consciously into the innermost third circle, the circle of *Who*.

When I move inward toward the center of myself, I move closer to the person I most truly am before God. This is dangerous ground. As I begin to see who I am—truly and without protective masks—I may find serious discrepancies between the person who lives in the Where and the person God created me to be, in my deepest self. I will find shame, but I will also find glory. I will move closer to the God who dwells in my heart, and the encounter will challenge me in ways I cannot predict. This is the power of prayer. It is the risk of the inner journey.

Growing the Godseed

Now imagine that the circles have sprouted leaves and flowers. These are not just for decoration. My own experience tells me that when I make the journey inward, or, rather, when I allow God to penetrate my center—what we commonly call our "heart"—a powerful creative act takes place. I call it the germination of my "Godseed."

What exactly is a Godseed, and what causes it to germinate? As Christians, we talk about God as being both immanent (present to us, individually and collectively, in our hearts and in our human experience) and transcendent (utterly beyond our reach or imagination, totally "other" and without limits). My Godseed, I believe, is nothing less than the immanent God at rest in my heart, waiting to be expressed in an act of germination, of resurrection.

How does the germination happen? There are countless ways, and we can never pin God down by trying to define how God will act. One way of visualizing this mystery is to notice moments when we seem to be in contact with something, or someone, beyond ourselves; it may feel like a tangent touching the outer circle of our lives. We know, at times like these, that something has happened that is different from the normal run of our daily lives, though not separated from it. We might feel as if we have been touched by God. It could have happened in all sorts of ways — through intense communion with nature or in a human relationship, in a moment of deep insight that seemed to come from beyond ourselves, or perhaps in a sudden clarity that showed us the way forward in a particular situation.

When these moments happen, we could say that God has not only "touched" us but has somehow "taken root" in our lived experience. That touch of Life will, if we allow it, penetrate down through the layers of our experience until it reaches the center. There, the transcendent God who touched us will join with the immanent God locked up, like a seed, in our hearts, and something new will grow from that union. We could imagine a flower (or plant or bush or tree) that will be the unique manifestation (or incarnation) of God that is ours, and ours alone, to bring forth. If we do not bring it to birth, it will not come to birth. If we do, it can become the realization of God's dream for us. It is the inner mystery of ourselves that is already known—that has always been known—to God, that he is longing to bring to fulfillment.

Bringing God's dream for us to birth is the amazing vocation of every believer. We might reflect at this point on Mary's response to the Annunciation and acknowledge that moment in ourselves when God asks, "Are you willing to bring me to birth in your own life?" and our response is, "Let it be done to me according to your will."

Prayer as Sabbath Time

Suppose, then, that germination has happened. How can we bring God's dream to reality? I suggest that we can cooperate in this act, consciously and deliberately, in prayer, because prayer takes us to our Who

Prayer is . . .

- not just a linear journey through the days of our lives
- but a radial journey into the deep heart of ourselves
- and then out again through our How
- bringing the seeds of transformation into our Where

center. Through prayer we allow God to nourish our Godseed, and we ourselves are nourished by it. The profound understanding and reverence the Jews have for the Sabbath can help us to see prayer in a different perspective. For the Jew, the Sabbath is not for the sake of the weekdays; it is not an interlude for recreation to enable us to work all the harder during the week. Rather, the weekdays are for the sake of the Sabbath. The Sabbath is not just a break in the pattern of daily life but the whole meaning of it.

In the same way, prayer is not just a means of sustaining us through our linear journey (though it does that, too) but is itself the reality of our journey. It is not primarily a calm interlude in our day, a "quiet time," but the very essence of our being. When we are at prayer, we are most truly who we are, and we are at prayer whenever we are really "living true." In later chapters we will look at how to recognize and foster this state of living true.

Seen in this light, prayer is time taken out of the linear journey of our days, and it is also our most profound reality. When we pray, we move inward to our God center. Then we move out again, back through the layers of our How, to our Where situation in the world. This movement into the center and out again brings about an act of transformation. This is not to say that we will come out of prayer transfigured, like Jesus on the mountain (though our prayer experience may sometimes be dramatic). Nothing so spectacular! Usually there is a subtle, gentle, almost indiscernible change in our way of being that will carry its healing, changing power out through the layers of our lived experience and infuse the Where of our lives with its Kingdom values. This happens every time we pray, whether we are aware of it or not.

When we open ourselves to God in prayer, we invite him to enter our Who center, bringing the gifts of the Spirit into the heart of our lived experience, with all its problems, pain, and sin. As the transforming

work is done, the Spirit in turn carries our needs and longings, and the
needs and longings of all those for whom we pray, back to the heart of
God. These are not just flights of wishful fancy. These are the promises
God made to us, through his Son, and our lived experience testifies to
their truth and their validity.

Before we leave the circles (which are only convenient images to try
to capture something of what it is to be a believing human being), you
might like to look at a few variations on what it might mean to deepen
our perception of things from the outermost, surface level of response
to the deepest responses in the center of ourselves, such as:

- the deepening of mere pleasure and pain through happiness and
  unhappiness, to joy and sorrow,
- the deepening of prayer itself from vocal or liturgical prayer
  through personal confession and meditation, to contemplative
  union with God,
- the passage from the transience of mere feelings, through the
  fidelity of faith, to the fact of God's unchanging love,
- the movement from being a person to whom things happen,
  through the realization that we can influence what happens, to
  the acceptance of personal responsibility for being an event who
  happens to others,
- the movement from obsession with our immediate wants and fears
  through the acceptance of responsibility in community and relationship, to the intimacy and trust of nonpossessive love.

In each of these contexts (and I'm sure you can think of many
more), you will notice an outer layer that could be compared to the
Where experience, a deeper layer corresponding to the How response,
and an innermost center accessible only to our Who reality.

This deepening, from Where through How to Who is the hallmark
of all personal prayer — perhaps especially so in the Ignatian tradition,
which encourages us to begin by finding God in the ordinary outward
things of our lived experience and to allow that discovery to draw us
down to his deepest meanings for our life and growth in him.

The "Weeks" of Our Hearts

In his *Exercises,* Ignatius invites the pilgrim to follow a framework of prayer that he divides into four "weeks." These are not weeks of the seven-day variety and are not intended to map onto calendar weeks. Rather, they are phases or stages through which the pray-er will move, following this framework, and everyone who "completes" the *Exercises* realizes that "in the end is the beginning." A person coming to the end of the Fourth Week of prayer may well discover, for example, frequent reconnections to the prayer of the First Week.

It is one of the hidden graces of the *Exercises* that we get in touch with these many different "weeks" within ourselves, in the inner movements of our hearts, and that we come to realize their total interconnectedness. We don't have to progress neatly from fallenness to resurrection in our life with God. The pattern of redemption isn't a straight line or even a wavy line. It isn't even really a circle, because each time we reconnect to our beginnings, the connection is different, and the circle is redrawn in a new and different way.

This pattern, which sounds so mysterious when we attempt to describe it in words, is actually as simple and as beautiful as the earth itself. On the surface and above, there is the weather. It is constantly changing, yet each kind of weather bears its own gifts — some welcome, some less so. Sometimes the weather is extreme and out of order; sometimes it is moderate and balanced. In its unreliability it feels just like us, with our moods and feelings.

Then there is the layer of topsoil, very much influenced by our "weather" but more stable and carrying the Godseed for germination and growth. This is our heart soil, where God is growing his Kingdom.

And under the soil is the bedrock. Whenever we go deep in prayer, or into relationship with God and with each other, or into the mystery and meaning of things, we will eventually come up against this hard rock. It can feel like the solid door of a locked room. There is no way out, no way in. It is so dark that we don't even rightly know whether we are trying to get in (to a treasure chamber) or out (of a prison cell). Maybe both. Yet God is the bedrock, just as he is in our weather and in our soil. The rock is his unwavering holding of us, the solid foundation without which we would sink into the quicksand. But it is also the hard rock that shatters us when we fall upon it and that breaks us open, as it broke God himself upon the cross.

That rock opens up, from time to time, in our inner vision—glimpse-wise and terrifyingly—as it did when Jesus uttered, "It is completed!" and as it does for us sometimes in the dreadful movements of our inner earthquakes. From the silent, secret shafts of burning light that occasionally streak through prayer or dream, we know that beneath the bedrock is an ever blazing fire. This is the molten center of ourselves, the source of our passion and energy. Like our surface weather, it is sometimes wild and disordered, sometimes creative and life giving. This same inner fire is also the fire of God at the heart of all his creation. Sometimes we dread it, because it has the aspect of the flames of hell. Sometimes we long for it, because it seems to be alight with the very splendor of God's eternal presence and the radiance of heaven.

These four layers—the weather, the soil, the rock, and the fire—are also vivid images of the four "weeks" of the *Exercises*:

- The weather of ourselves, our moods and feelings, our dependency on God, our finiteness, our unreliability, and our fragmented nature are all topics for the prayer of the First Week. Now rain, now sunshine, storm, and glory, our life's weather is insubstantial in itself, yet it is affected by the deepest movements of our hearts, and affects every other creature on the earth. It reveals the brokenness of sin, spanned by the rainbow of an unconditional love.

- Then the soil of our growing, learning, listening, sitting at the feet of the Lord, imbibing his goodness; sharing in his earthly ministry; becoming, in him, the person we truly are; taking root, following our deepest desire, striving up to the light, being pruned and tended . . . the Second Week.

- Then the splintering, shattering rock. The breaking open and the breaking down. The Calvary journey, with the Lord and in ourselves . . . the Third Week.

> **Freedom happens . . .**
>
> • not by moving from one spot on the Where circle to another
> • but by moving into the Who center, in God's presence, and allowing ourselves to be "dipped in God,"
> • then returning to the Where in a transformed way, to make that part of our world a little bit more free

• And then, the earthquake of "It is completed!" Earth splits open, and its heart fire flows free, consuming and destroying or quickening and energizing. It destroys all that is not truth and transcends truth into life. The fire of the Spirit breaks open the locked space of the tomb in the Fourth Week.

And in the end is the beginning. The explosion of resurrection energy at the heart of things changes the surface weather forever, and the weather affects the soil, and the roots of our Godseed touch the bedrock of God's love, and the cycle continues, but always differently, always uniquely. And when all cycles are fulfilled, the Kingdom is.

The Search for Freedom

Finally, a word about freedom. We will be looking at what "inner freedom" might mean in more depth in a later chapter. However, while we are with the circles, it is worth noticing what inner freedom does and does not mean in terms of our journey to the Who center.

The temptation is to seek freedom by moving from one spot on the Where circle to another. I suppose I would be free (and therefore, fulfilled and happy) if I were not in this place (in this relationship, in this job, etc.), and so I will seize my freedom by moving. What happens, if we do this, is that we exchange one unfreedom for another. We uproot our Godplant and expect it to flourish better elsewhere.

A second possibility is to move not sideways but inward, into the Who center, taking all the pain of our unfreedom with us and allowing ourselves to be "dipped in God" (as D. H. Lawrence describes it). Then we will return to the same place on our Where circle but in a transformed way, however slightly. The result will be to make that part of our Where a little bit more free.

This is not to deny that a change of circumstances can sometimes be necessary and beneficial. But it is to say that real and permanent change and transformation happen in the Who and not in the Where of ourselves. Changing the Where may well free us *from* something that we find oppressive or destructive, and sometimes that may be a necessary stage in our journey. But the deepest purpose of transformation is to free us *for* something, and that something is nothing less than the coming of the Kingdom, our own personal resurrection, and the resurrection of the whole human family.

SUGGESTIONS FOR PRAYER AND REFLECTION   1

In the sixth month the angel Gabriel was sent by God to a town in Galilee called Nazareth, to a virgin betrothed to a man named Joseph, of the House of David; and the virgin's name was Mary. He went in and said to her, "Rejoice, so highly favored! The Lord is with you." She was deeply disturbed by these words and asked herself what this greeting could mean, but the angel said to her, "Mary, do not be afraid; you have won God's favor. Listen! You are to conceive and bear a son, and you must name him Jesus. He will be great and will be called Son of the Most High. The Lord God will give him the throne of his ancestor David; he will rule over the House of Jacob for ever and his reign will have no end." Mary said to the angel, "But how can this come about, since I am a virgin?" "The Holy Spirit will come upon you," the angel answered, "and the power of the Most High will cover you with its shadow. And so the child will be holy and will be called Son of God. Know this too: your kinswoman Elizabeth has, in her old age, herself conceived a son, and she whom people called barren is now in her sixth month, for nothing is impossible to God."

"I am the handmaid of the Lord," said Mary, "let what you have said be done to me." And the angel left her.   (Luke 1:26–38)

TRY TO IMAGINE yourself as part of this scene. Paint a picture in your mind of the surroundings, the houses, the fields, the village, the weather, the sights and sounds and smells of the place. Are you a by-stander, or alongside Mary, or are you alone there?

Imagine the arrival of the angel. Hear his words. Notice your reaction. Ask God to open your heart to hear and understand anything God may wish to reveal to you, personally, in this scene. Be still, and let his meanings arise unobstructed to your consciousness, and respond to them in whatever way feels right for you.

USE A SHEET of blank concentric circles and fill in anything you find helpful about your own personal Where circumstances or about the way your How circle is forming as a result of decisions you have made in your life. Make a note of those things you cannot change and face your feelings about them. Look back over the past day, or perhaps the past week, and recall any moments of decision. How did you react to them? Where do you feel that your choices were made in a you-centered way, and where were they God centered? How do you feel about them now? You may like to tell God, in prayer, how you feel about them and show God anything you would like to change.

RECALL ANY EVENTS or relationships in your life when you have tried, or wanted, to achieve "freedom" by moving to a different point on the Where circle. Did you find the freedom you were seeking? Do you recall any times when you have stayed in a difficult situation, perhaps feeling imprisoned? How did you respond to that situation at the time? Would you react differently now? Bring your memories, including any regrets, to God, and show him, without fear, how you are feeling. Ask him con-fidently for healing and for the freedom you are seeking.

REFLECT ON GOD'S DREAM for you, the fruit of your Godseed, which is rooted in your relationship with him, in your Who center, but blossoms and bears fruit in the Where of your life. Let yourself be, in imagination, the flower (or plant or tree) that you are becoming. Now let yourself be in the roots. Feel them pushing down, deeper and deeper, toward the groundwater and God. Feel the sap rising through you, thrusting its way to fulfillment.

CAN YOU RECALL any moments when you have felt touched by God in the kind of way that has brought your Godseed to life? Remember these moments now in prayer and thank God for them. Ask him to show you how they have indeed been bringing about the fulfillment of his dream for you.

2

FINDING OUR PAST IN GOD

THE STORY IS told in the Old Testament (1 Kings 19) of how the prophet Elijah called Elisha to be his successor. Elisha's response seems ambivalent; he wants to follow, but he also wants to say good-bye to his family. Eventually, after some hesitation, Elisha takes the step of commitment, accepts the mantle of prophecy from Elijah, and follows.

A companion who was accompanying me for a while on my faith journey suggested this passage as a scriptural focus for my own prayer one day during a retreat. I have no doubt, with hindsight, that he was expecting the Lord to touch my heart, through this passage, into a less ambivalent kind of discipleship for myself. In fact, however, the passage affected me in a quite different way, which took us both by surprise.

My attention was captured by the picture of the eleven teams of oxen plowing the field ahead of Elisha, who was plowing with the twelfth and final team in the line. I knew that this picture had touched on something at a deeper level than my conscious thought, so I stayed with it and let it form my prayer that day. I noticed that it released a deep feeling of peace within me, as if I had recognized something important there. It seemed to speak to me of a calling that was not simply about my own response to God but about the whole continuum of human response to the divine. Specifically, it seemed to be a call for me to recognize those particular "oxen teams" who have provided the guidance and the pulling power for me in the plowing of my life's furrow, those men and women who were personal beacons for me on my journey of faith.

You might like to join me in my retrospective meditation. Begin by imagining yourself standing outside your own home, beneath a brilliant, starry sky. Take in the splendor and the immense space stretching out above you, beyond your grasp, beyond measurement. Out of reach and utterly transcendent, stars are an image of the infinite yet are connected to us as surely as we are connected to every other created thing.

Now find a familiar constellation. Out of the infinity, there is something recognizable — it pinpoints your location exactly in time and space. Feel the thrill of claiming your unique place within the vast heart of God.

Now hear the word of Scripture. Elijah is calling Elisha to the life of a prophet of the Lord . . .

> Leaving there, he came to Elisha son of Shaphat as he was plowing behind twelve yoke of oxen, he himself being with the twelfth. Elijah passed near to him and threw his cloak over him.   (1 Kings 19:19)

Imagine yourself in a field. The field is being plowed, and you have your own furrow to plow. The field is the field of the world, where you are plowing the furrow of your life. Your hands are on the plow, and your feet are heavy with the earth. Perhaps you feel that you are carrying out this gigantic task all alone. But look ahead of you. See the eleven teams of oxen that Elisha saw. You are not alone. You are part of a long line of life and of meaning. But this is not just any line of oxen teams. This is your own personal line, plowing your particular furrow.

Who or what is in your line of oxen teams? Think of significant people who have made an important difference in your life. Some of them may be among the first disciples and saints. Some may be in your recent past. Some may be walking alongside you today. These are people who have helped to form the line of your life, your furrow. They have helped to provide the pulling power for your plow and to guide its progress.

Not just people, but important moments, events, decisions, or experiences will have formed your furrow. Remember them. See how they have moved you on or possibly corrected your direction.

Notice the landscape of your part of the field, the places that have been important to you.

If you ask a farmer how he ensures that he is plowing a straight furrow, he will give you this advice: Fix your eyes straight ahead, on some fixed point on the horizon—a tree perhaps—and keep moving steadily toward it. Don't watch the furrow. Just keep your hands on the plow and your eyes on that fixed point.

Jesus is our fixed point. He is at the head of each one of our personal lines of oxen teams. It is his risen life and energy that provide the power for our every movement. But he gives us, too, our own personal constellation of people (past and present) and landmarks and signposts for our unique journey.

Let your journey bring you back to your place beneath the stars. Remember your line of earthly oxen teams and see them as a reflection of God's personal shaping of your life, mapped out in the infinity of his heart.

Like the stars, they can locate you firmly on the solid ground of your own life, and they can reveal much to you about your journey. They can help you find your way. They can be channels to you of that driving energy of the risen Christ, who is always your pulling power and your destination.

When you look back over the line of people and events that have shaped your life, you are also looking forward to your destination because Christ is truly the beginning and the end, the Alpha and Omega of your own being.

Gently return to your place in the here and now, strong in the knowledge that you do not plow the field alone and that the story of your life will lead you back through your special landmarks to the Lord himself, the Lord of your harvest.

The River Mee

If you are not moved to plow fields, you might find a gentler image more helpful. You might reflect on your life as resembling the flow of a river, from its first beginnings in a hidden, secret source to its outflowing into the ocean of its destination.

I remember a marvelous weekend I once spent with relatives in Scotland. They had just moved to a new home in the Scottish Borders. One Saturday they took us out for a drive to show us their new surroundings, and we came across a sign that marked the source of a river—that elusive, indefinable point where the waters gather and a new thing begins. "This is the source of the River Tweed," the sign read. I'd never seen such a sign before, probably because it is extraordinarily difficult to locate exactly where a river has its source, just as it is difficult to define exactly when a new human life begins. For a river, as for an embryo, there is that vague, invisible time of not-quite-thereness, where waters are gathering, cells are multiplying, and there is a hint of something—someone—new that may or may not come to fulfillment.

Our outing on that day seemed, from then on, to be defined by that chance meeting with the sign marking the river's source. In the speed and comfort of the car, we traveled in minutes a journey of forever, from the ever springing, never-quite-discernible source, down the trickling burn, along the gathering river. In minutes, the almost-nothing source was a river where fishermen sat, dipping their boots into trout-fertile waters, where trees sprang and rooted, giving leaf cover, shade, and fruit in due season. The hidden source had, that quickly, become a stately presence in the valley town, spanned by a proud, wide bridge, humming with Saturday people and the plaintive song of the bagpipes.

From the wild unknown of a secret source, we soon came to the tamed and admired that could be named and lived alongside, fished and bridged and celebrated, before it spilled into the boundless, unnamed and unnameable ocean. We experienced the telescoped adventure of a forever journey.

For the River Tweed, you might like to substitute the River Mee, and reflect on the course of your personal river so far and on where you think or hope or dream that it might be leading.

The river makes a difference to the landscape through which it flows. It carves its way through the earth—hard clay or soft sand—where it finds itself; it finds ways to go beyond the obstructions and blockages that it meets; it may flow underground, forming channels and caves, or it may spread out and water the land around it. And the relationship with the land is reciprocal, because the landscape also makes a difference to how the river flows and where its destination is to be. The landscape gives the contours that determine the water's journey; it offers space for the flow or resists it; it cooperates with the power of the water or it struggles against it.

This is only a metaphor, of course, but you may find that some reflection on the relationship of your own life's river with its given landscape reveals much about who you really are, what influences are forming you, what you welcome in your story and what you fight against, and above all, what you dream of becoming as you widen and deepen toward your destination. This is the landscape of your circumstances, your origins, your family and friends, those people who have been important in your life, those events that have pointed out new directions to you, the difficulties you have had to negotiate and those aspects of the scene that have given you energy and joy.

Like my drive along the River Tweed, your reflections may cover in minutes what has been evolving since the moment you were conceived. And conversely, they may lend timeless significance to the passing moments of your daily life if you flow on with open eyes. Consider, for example:

- What do you know and value of your own origins?

- What kind of landscape has your river flowed through so far?

- What kinds of obstructions or hazards has it had to negotiate?

- Have you ever felt that your river's energy and power were being sapped and exploited by others?

- Has your life river ever appeared to disappear? To go underground or to dry up? To lose itself in the bog lands or marshes of your experience?
- What detours do you see, with hindsight, that your life has made?
- How and where do you feel that your river is flowing now?
- As you let your mind wander back along the riverbanks you have known, what landmarks make you feel glad and grateful? Perhaps particular people or experiences? Have you ever told those concerned what a difference they made to your journey?
- What landmarks have left you feeling angry, disappointed, misled, betrayed, or in any way negative? If other people were involved in these situations in your life, do you still harbor resentments against them, or can you now turn around to focus on the future rather than on the past? Are there things you would like to talk over with the people concerned? Do you feel able to do so? (Do so only if you really feel comfortable about it.)

Your Faith Story

A faith story (or faith biography) is simply an account of your inner journey through the outer events of your life. It is the story of how you have gradually (or suddenly) become aware of a relationship with God and the ways in which he has been leading you. It is a kind of inner map of the feelings life has roused in you, the decisions you have made along the way, and the way you have made them. It would include significant landmarks along the way where you feel that something grew inside you, and significant people who have walked alongside you at different stages of your journey and brought you closer to an understanding of yourself.

And how to do it?

One way to approach your faith story might be through one of the pictures we have looked at: the eleven teams of oxen or the River Mee. Your faith story would simply be an expression of what those pictures have revealed to you.

Why write your faith story?

- It puts you in touch with the most important events and people of your life and helps you notice the inner movements that reveal how God is touching you.
- It draws your life and your prayer together, to help you see every event and feeling of your lived experience as an invitation to deepen your relationship with God.
- It helps you say to God, "Here I am. This is how I feel I have become who I am. Let us journey on together toward who I shall become in you."

This isn't a literary exercise. Your faith story is a very personal conversation between you and God. If you find it easy to write, you might like to write it out, perhaps in the form of an account of those events and moments in your life that were charged with special feelings— good and bad—for you. Or you may prefer to use drawings or symbols to express those things that have been important to you; some people find it helpful to use different colors to represent their emotions with regard to these events.

You should feel free to tell your story in whatever way or ways are natural and meaningful for you. What is important is for you to get in touch with the movements in your life and with your feelings about your life, and by doing this, to get in touch with the ways in which God has been present to you in it.

Your faith story is yours alone. However, you may wish to share it, in part at least, with someone you trust and feel comfortable with. (The Celts had a word for such a person; they called him or her an *anam-chara,* meaning "soul-friend"). To share your story in this way can help you to recognize the patterns and movements that it reveals, which in turn can help you to discern the ways in which God is present to your ongoing journey.

When you have expressed your story, as you see it now, keep it in a safe place without changing anything. From time to time, go back to it, and see for yourself how it has moved on, which patterns and movements have become stronger, and how you feel then about the areas of light and darkness, the joyful and sorrowful mysteries of your life. You may find that some of the sorrowful mysteries were in fact the places and the times when God was drawing you closer to him, drawing you into his own suffering, or inviting you to grow beyond the hurts that have held you to the past.

Finally, enjoy the exercise. Let your joys be joys, and let your sorrows be brought into a healing light.

The End of the Furrow

I have lived with the reality of my eleven teams of oxen for several years now, since the picture first suggested itself to me. But today I feel I know something of its ending. Even as I write, a dear friend is standing on the brink of death, surrounded by his wife and family. There may be a call at any minute to say that he has left us.

It's the first of May, and the world is burgeoning with springtime. Everywhere, the blossoms hang so rich and heavy on the trees that you can almost taste the cherries. The oak trees are leafing early this year, and life is bursting its seams. It is also the feast day of St. Joseph, the worker and faithful husband, God's foster father. My friend has been like a father to me—a spiritual father.

Here in Britain, it is the day of the general election, a day that the politicians have called a day of destiny, and one when many are hoping for a new start under a new government, with a new vision of peace and social justice, a vision that was part of my friend's driving inspiration. This is a day full of promise and hope, but my heart aches for my dying friend. Yet he has lived a long and deeply fruitful life, and my tears are charged with the knowledge that what he has given to me and to so many others is not for grieving over, or even for holding on to, but for living out and for handing on.

He is one of my oxen teams. He has walked ahead of me in the field, showing the straight furrow, drawing me by the power of his own faith, and urging me to keep going and to keep my gaze focused on the fixed point on the horizon that marks the heart of our destination. Very soon he will become part of that destination. I thank him, even as I weep.

When Elijah came to the end of his furrow, he was taken up into heaven in a whirlwind. Elisha was told that if he were to continue plowing faithfully in the spirit of the one who had gone before, and to receive the flame from the one who had run the race ahead of him, he must have the courage to watch steadily as Elijah was taken up to heaven.

When I first came across this story, I took it to be simply the dramatic account of an exceptionally charismatic prophet. Now I feel sure that it is a call to all of us. We each have our line of oxen teams, and I hope that in this chapter you have been able to get in touch with some of your own. We all draw energy and guidance from the personal wisdom figures who have plowed ahead of us along our personal furrow. We are all called to watch steadily, just as a relay runner stays alert to the approach of the one who will hand the baton to him to carry forward, or as an Olympic torchbearer watches as his turn approaches to carry the flame onward for the next lap of the journey home. If we watch steadily, we will plow sure and straight, and the energies of love, life, and wisdom that have guided us will pass in some way into and through our own hearts. It is given to us not just for our own sake but also for the sake of those who will follow after.

MY FRIEND HAS died now. He doesn't teach anymore—he is. And that, surely, is how God teaches us, by *being*. Perhaps this change, when it starts to happen in ourselves, marks the transition from disciple to apostle—from one who listens and learns to one who turns what is being learned into what is being lived. This happens when you, once the twelfth in your line of oxen teams, find that the baton has passed on to you and that you yourself are being asked to take on your share of responsibility for providing the guidance and transmitting the pulling power to the ones who follow after.

And so I commend to you the task of discerning your faith story, for it is a sacred task. Learn to know your oxen teams, and be thankful for them. Watch with steady courage the ones who plow ahead of you, and receive in faith and love the flame they place into your hands.

SUGGESTIONS FOR PRAYER AND REFLECTION   2

Remembering . . .

During the next few weeks, take a little time in prayer to remember your life—your journey of faith so far—in God's presence.

> *Re-member-ing* means, literally, piecing together again what has become fragmented or broken. Ask God for the grace to re-member the fragments of your life in a way that will reveal to you the patterns that are leading toward your wholeness in him.

Try the following exercises:

- Remember the exterior events of your life and your reactions to them. As you remember these events, notice the gifts that you have received: skills and talents, gifts of personality, gifts from your circumstances—education, family, friends, jobs, your whole situation in life, gifts of people who have become significant for you.

- Notice now how God has been constantly present, not just in the special moments. Notice especially how, with hindsight, periods when he felt absent may have prepared you in some way for further growth. Notice how periods of difficulty strengthened you in certain ways, as hard exercise strengthens our muscles. Remember how consolation and new strength have sometimes come when you were at the end of the line. This isn't to pretend to yourself that everything, with hindsight, was good. That would be dishonest and untrue, because we live in a fallen world where evil is endemic. Where honesty prevents you from seeing God in parts of your life, tell him so in your prayer, and express your pain and anger to him freely.

- Become aware of how God touches your unique personality and brings you to life, how he speaks to you through your own personality, your gifts, and your decisions. Can you see any concrete examples of how God is using your gifts or working through your decisions now, in your immediate experience?

- Try to describe—or to draw—your own images of God. How does he appear to you—a father figure, a policeman, a friend, a doctor, a male or female, distant or close, firm or gentle, judging, guiding, or apparently ignoring you? It may be helpful to remember how you thought of God when you were a child and compare those images with the way you see him now. Your childhood images may actually express more honestly what you still, deep down, truly feel. There is no one right answer. The purpose of the exercise is to get in touch with the way you are personally relating to God and with how you feel about that relationship.

At every point, express your feelings to God in prayer, without fear and without holding anything back.

To use Scripture in prayer, read the passage through carefully until you feel at home with it, and ask the Lord to open your heart to discern its personal meanings for you and your own life's journey. This is the basis of all scriptural prayer.

The passages suggested below may help you to explore particular aspects of your own story, with the Lord alongside you. They are only suggestions, so use them only if they are helpful. If you find yourself especially drawn toward a particular passage (one of these or any other), stay with it. You can be sure that God is wanting to reveal something to you through it. Repeat it as often as you feel drawn to do so. Go back especially to any point where you experienced any kind of strong feeling. These strong feelings (negative or positive) are signs of deep inner movements in your heart and may be pointers to where God is acting in your life. They are signals to you that this is an area that should be looked at more closely. Repetition like this can lead to great deepening and healing of a particular aspect of your life. People have been known to spend the whole of an eight-day retreat praying with just one passage that was crucial to their growth.

The Creation of Human Life   GENESIS 1:26–31

Reflect on your own beginnings, the "garden" in which your life has been planted. Notice how God's creating energy and joy have been bringing you to life in so many different ways since you were first conceived.

Notice verse 31 in particular and receive its affirmation personally into your heart.

The Birth of Moses   EXODUS 2:1–10

Reflect on your early years of growth and change. Let the Lord lead you through any dark experiences of loss, fear, danger, or threat. Moses was born into an extremely threatening situation. Are there "bulrush" times in your experience? Can you trace, with hindsight, the hand of God in the ways you were brought through them?

Where, in the end, was the greater power: in the basket made of reeds or in the might of Pharaoh's empire?

Reflect on how God's promise to Moses was brought to fulfillment, and reflect on the promise he has implanted in your own life.

The Pillar of Cloud
and the Pillar of Fire   EXODUS 13:17–22

Desert times can be times of wandering, directionless survival or even despair, times when you seem to be going round in circles and getting nowhere. Open up your own desert spaces in prayer, and ask the Lord to show you how to recognize your own pillars of cloud and fire in the confusion.

Notice that Moses carries the body of Joseph, the dreamer, across the wilderness to the Promised Land. We, too, are invited to carry our dreams through our deserts. Notice the dreams that God is asking you to carry, and carry them joyfully.

The Call of Elisha   1 KINGS 19:19

You may like to get in touch with your own "eleven teams of oxen" if this image is helpful.

Reflect in prayer on the events, circumstances, and people that have led you further along your path of growth and helped you to plow your furrow. Then see the Lord at their head, and feel his Spirit running through your personal line of meaning.

Lord, You Have Examined Me
and You Know Me   PSALM 139:1–16

Hear the words of the psalm applied to the days of your own life. Reflect on the thoughts expressed in verses 13, 15, and 16, on the infinite value to God of your being, even when you were "being formed in secret" in your mother's womb. Now reflect on the infinite value to God of your inner being, which even now is "being formed in secret" at the heart of your lived experience.

Ask the Lord to lead you in prayer to share something of his own deep knowledge of you, that knowledge all of us long for yet often seek to avoid.

When you recall the dark and the light times of your own experience, let the words of verse 12 set them into perspective for you.

The Samaritan Woman   JOHN 4:5–30

Imagine yourself going to the well to draw the day's water. Encounter Jesus there, a stranger who knows you through and through. Let him engage you in conversation, and let him take you in that conversation wherever he will.

Then return to the village. What difference has the encounter made to your future journeying?

Walk to Emmaus   LUKE 24:13–35

Place yourself in imagination alongside the two disciples in their bewildered disappointment. Allow the stranger to come alongside you. He seems to know nothing about the events of your life, so tell him how it has been for you. Tell him how you are feeling about the course of your life so far, your hopes, your fears, and your expectations.

When you reach the crossroads . . . what happens next?

3 ⊚

So What Went Wrong?

WE HAVE SPENT time exploring some elusive questions. "Who am I?" "What is the real heart of me all about?" "What has shaped me into the person I am today?" I hope that you have discovered something of the trace of God's finger in everything that has made you "you," and in everything that is continuing to shape you into who you really are.

Yet we live in what seems to be a broken world, and our lives are blighted by an abiding sense of being separated from our source, alienated from our true selves and from each other. Each one of us, today, can look back over what can seem (in the bad times) like a trail of broken dreams and shattered hopes. Or perhaps our hidden Godseed appears to have amounted to nothing more exciting than a middle-aged couch potato.

In the first stage of the *Spiritual Exercises,* Ignatius invites the pilgrim to reflect on what we might call "the scale of the problem." What does "fallenness" really mean in our lived experience? Can it be that God loves us unconditionally, through it and beyond it all, or is that just wishful thinking?

To know the reality of our brokenness and our separation from God, in our gut and not just in our heads, is a harrowing experience. We enter into this experience only when we know, in the same deep-felt way,

So what went wrong? Can we be satisfied by the conventional religious language of "sin" and somehow make that cover for the inner howling that comes from the deep awareness of something badly wrong, that no amount of theology is going to cure for us?

God's unconditional love for us, which holds our brokenness in gently sheltering hands.

Discovering the Godseed in our hearts, noticing the golden threads of meaning in our own life's journey, and becoming increasingly aware of God's continuing presence in our lives and in everything and everyone we encounter are just a few of the possibilities for opening ourselves up more and more to this unconditional love, even as we stand face-to-face with the nature and extent of our own fallenness and the fallenness of all creation.

A couple of parables from my own life's journey have helped me to make this connection between God's free-flowing love for us, and our own imprisonment in our own, and the world's, brokenness.

Lock 46

Many years ago, I worked in a place not far from the Trent and Mersey canal. During lunch breaks, I would often wander through the surrounding fields, down to the towpath, and walk along the canal for a while. In those days there was a good deal less pressure at work, and extended lunch hours were a luxury we tended to take for granted.

All kinds of unpleasantness have intervened between those happy memories and the place where I find myself today, including the loss of that job and the relative security it once held for me. Some of that unpleasantness was undoubtedly of my own making. Some of it seems to be endemic to the way life hurts everyone in some way or other as the years go on.

As chance (or God?) would have it, however, I found myself back there recently, sent by my present employer, an agency, to carry out a short-term contract in the place where I had once been a "permanent" employee. One lunchtime when the sun was shining, I decided that I would risk a half-hour absence from my contractor's desk, because I suddenly had the urge to go back through the fields of my memory and seek out the canal towpath again. The walk, stolen out of the middle of a hectic day, became a prayer and gave me a perspective on my own life's journey that permanently changed my way of seeing things.

It was a lovely, warm, mellow October day. The clouds were scudding across a pale blue sky, and the leaves collected in floating brown islands by the lock gates. Lock 46, as the sign read, became my place of rest for a space, a million miles away from the unreal realities of the office. It was a dappled day, and the sunlight warmed my heart into responsiveness, like a lover's touch. "My peace I give you," the unspoken words reverberated, "not as the world gives."

From time to time a canal narrow boat passed through the lock. It amazed me how this gently flowing water, so peaceful in the autumn sunshine, suddenly took on the power to raise several tons of iron and steel by all those feet between where I was sitting and the deep drop to the lock floor. And I knew, as I watched, that God is doing the same for me. His Spirit flows so gently and unobtrusively through the landscape of my heart, but when its power is called for, it can raise me from the depths of my unfreedom to the heights of his love, and free me to continue my journey, borne on this fragile flow that seems so ephemeral yet runs eternally.

I let the breeze caress me, and it told the same kind of truth. It's only the breeze that reminds me that there is air all around me. I only notice its presence when it is stirred by storm and currents. It was a gentle breeze that day, just enough to flick the clouds into playfulness and rustle the dying leaves. Yet it carried the seeds of next year's springtime, and its every molecule surrounded me with the oxygen I need to stay alive. What unseen powers are these, in wind and water, all sunshine-dappled and charged with an energy that is capable of setting a universe in motion, but also with a love that is able—and desiring—to touch my heart into peace?

But I had extended my lunch break too far already. I made my way back, past a contemplative fisherman who was surely reaching for his own peace as well. The notice on the canal sign by the pub read, "48-hour moorings only." This week had put that notice up in my life, too. Here I was, just a contractor back in the place where I had worked for so many years. I was at a different desk each day, wherever there happened to be space, using a borrowed laptop computer, plugged in wherever I could find a vacant socket. I knew hardly anyone here now, and hardly anyone knew me. The foxes have holes, and the birds of the air have nests, but a contract worker has nowhere to plug in her laptop, at least not for more than a 48-hour mooring!

It all reflected my deep sense of inner homelessness, but today it didn't disturb me. In fact, it stirred some deep desire to be with the water and the air in the life-bringing, power-in-gentleness of their flow and with the sunlight that filtered through the yellowing leaves to warm me into joy. I can't catch the water or hold the breeze or store up the sunlight, any more than I can be sure where my workplace will be tomorrow. But this graced hour, in the 48-hour mooring, seemed more real to me than all the structures I had thought were my life's harbor. There was peace in the flow, not the peace I might have sought in the strength of my own foolish wisdom, but the peace that God had set out before me in the wise folly of the falling leaves that settle for a moment on the water that flows through Lock 46 and then are gone.

All this had been a lived, and felt, experience of God's unconditional love.

But perhaps the most far-reaching grace of this lunchtime retreat to Lock 46 came when I realized that I myself feel rather like a narrow boat in the lock chamber with the lock gates firmly closed on me. Because I have no real knowledge of what came before the lock chamber or what will follow after, the lock chamber itself seems to be all there is. I believe, in faith, that there is a canal that has brought me here and that will, in some mysterious way, take me further, but in my lived experience it usually doesn't feel like that. It often feels as though I am here in a deep, dark prison, facing brick walls on every side, and with no way out that my mind can guess at or imagine. This is a pointless and daunting place to be. If I think about my condition at all, I start to examine every brick or stone in that lock chamber, as if it were the whole arena of my living, in the hope that a minute examination of its walls might reveal some meaning in it or some way of dealing with it.

This process of examining my prison walls, though it may be absorbing, is ultimately rather futile, because it completely lacks perspective. The lock chamber makes no sense at all unless you know about the canal. Without the canal, the boat is truly just a prisoner in a pointless place. But when the reality of the canal is felt and embraced, then the transformation happens. Then the lock chamber is seen to be the place, and the only place, where God's grace might be flowing in to raise me to the place where I must be, if my homeward journey with him is to go on into what is still unexplored.

To raise me or to lower me? Sometimes, as I look back, I can see that grace has flowed into my empty lock and lifted me up, on its tide, into God's presence, with no effort of my own. But sometimes it seems to do just the opposite. Grace seems to be draining away, and I feel myself sinking lower and lower between the dark, damp stones, to be left alone in the very darkest depths of myself until God opens the lock gates and sets me free to journey on. Downstream or upstream? Either way transforms the dark imprisonment of the lock chamber of our lives into the very place that is making possible the onward movement on a journey that is infinitely larger and greater than our caged hearts can understand.

My fallenness, it seems to me, has something to do with this loss of perspective. It is about my feeling of the radical separation of myself from the flow of life, love, and God that alone makes sense of me. But the flow of God's love never ceases to be there for me, and even as I sit captive in my lock chamber, not knowing where I am or why, God is already manning the lock gates and bringing me, in his own time and his own way, to the point of readiness for moving on.

The Signpost City

Perhaps we begin to understand the nature of our imprisonment only when we have at least begun to be freed from it.

I lived for several years in Berlin during the time of the Cold War. Our flat was in a run-down inner-city area in the north of town, less than fifty meters from the Wall. We were often awakened at night by the sound of shots and the flash of flares. During this period we also experienced a blockade preventing the normal flow of traffic along any of the three land routes between West Berlin and West Germany. The only way for us to travel beyond the city limits in those years was to use one of the three air corridors to the West. Apart from that, Berlin at that time could be encapsulated on the subway map. This was a network of streets, squares, and junctions named after unknown places in the lost hinterland of East Germany that I could not even imagine.

It never occurred to me that these were anything more than names on a street plan. I walked the avenues and shopped in the squares. I traveled to work along the network. I could get onto the subway anywhere in West Berlin, and within half an hour I would hear the words, *"Endstation. Alle aussteigen."* "This is the end of the line. Please leave the train."

And it was so. Beyond the terminus was a no-man's-land with its watchtowers and mines, its Wall and its barbed wire, and its Full Stop.

This memory of Berlin returned to me very vividly one day in prayer. Suddenly I could see that I was like the beleaguered city, and that was exactly how I felt when I started to realize my separateness from God. I comprise a little space, a little bit of consciousness and choice, a little tangle of loving and fearing, longing and hiding, desiring and rejecting, but I am totally cut off from my hinterland. Like a besieged city, I am surrounded by unscalable walls and hostile guards; I am occupied by enemy forces. Only the air corridors of my prayer open up a slender connection to my eternal reality. Even my food and drink have to be airlifted to me, and if those supplies fail, I die.

Then my prayer led me on into the city itself. With these just-awakening eyes I began to see what was happening there. I had seen for myself that the city was an imprisoned, disconnected island, dependent upon supplies from outside for every morsel of food and every means of living. It was besieged by all the machinery of war and oppression, its captive inhabitants unable to go an inch beyond their tether. Yet that same city thinks it is the bastion of freedom! My city, my inner city, that depends on God just to stay in existence, also thinks it is both independent and free! Not only that, but it thinks it is some sort of model and defender of other people's freedom. Just as West Berlin set itself up (with American persuasion) as the "shop window of the West," so I can all too easily start to regard my inner city as if it were something for others to emulate.

The prayer humbled and mortified me and left me at God's feet in shame. For the first time, I could see the total absurdity and arrogance of my condition and, perhaps, of the whole human condition.

At first I could feel only the despair of the situation and my absolute helplessness in it. I felt my disconnectedness from God most deeply and horribly. My world, I realized, was built on quicksand, and it could collapse at any moment. Just as a Soviet blockade could have cut me off from bread and water, so the blockade of sin cuts me off from God . . . and I die. The logic is relentless.

In 1989, however, a miracle happened that nobody had really dared to hope for. The Berlin Wall came down. The whole country was opened up again, and it was possible, for the first time in over forty years, actually to go to the places that these so-familiar street names had pointed to. I shall never forget the discovery that the street names and subway stations I had known actually related to real places in the surrounding regions.

It was only as we drove through the towns and villages of Brandenburg and Mecklenburg that the subway map, my experience of Berlin, so completely circumscribed by circumstance, began to unfold, as a butterfly emerges from its awakening and tentatively spreads its damp wings. Every town and village connected to, and gave its name to, one of those familiar streets or squares or junctions. The end of the line wasn't a no-man's-land or an impassable barrier, but a real place, with houses, trees, cows and concrete, dustbins and maypoles, and all the sweat and tenderness of a living community. One after another, my subway stations came to life in these towns and villages of eastern Germany. The hinterland was the reality to which the enclosed, imprisoned city had been but the signpost.

It made me think differently about life and death. What if that shadowy mystery beyond the span of our years turns out to be the real country to which our earthly days are just the fragmented signposts? What if the unconscious realms in which our conscious minds are floating turn out to be the embryonic sac that is beckoning us toward a reality far beyond imagination? What if that of my life that seems so total, so final, and so absolute turns out to be the map into the hinterland of my eternal reality?

How reluctant we are to let go of the containing walls and risk a life beyond the circumscription. It seems easier to survive the slavery of Egypt than to venture into Sinai, and we convince ourselves that our slavery is freedom and our helplessness is a proud independence. The map changes radically when our walls come down and the real roads, that were always there, though impassable, are opened up. Then the hinterland becomes the heartland, where real life can really be lived.

My fallenness, I begin to understand, has a great deal to do with my determination to attend to the signposts and mistake them for the reality of things. I have become so attached to my wrong perceptions of what is real that I am blinded to the fullness of reality, to the extent that, if you show me a caterpillar, I will adamantly resist, and even ridicule, any suggestion that it contains a hidden butterfly. In my fallenness, I am equally blind to the possibility of my own embryonic butterfly and—even more seriously—I am blind to the butterfly in you.

Sin is, perhaps, like holding a daffodil bulb in our hands but neglecting to plant it in our life's soil because we refuse to believe that it contains a flower. Yet alongside all of our flat refusals to believe, the Gardener plants us nonetheless, and tends us lovingly because he knows who we are and holds everything we shall become in his gentle hands.

A Baby in the Minefield

Whatever is going to be necessary to redeem this fallenness, I slowly and painfully realize, is going to turn my own certainties and expectations upside down and inside out. The days of prayer that had taken me to Lock 46 and then back to Berlin now took me to the foot of the cross, where a man born to be king hung mangled and broken. He had come into the lost city, breaching its defenses from outside, and willingly joined himself to its despair and its lostness. He had come to lead me out, hopeless and bedraggled and mortally wounded, and carry me back home. He hung there because he had engaged the occupying forces on my behalf, and had conquered them.

But it didn't look like victory from where I was standing. It looked quite the opposite. Why was he hanging there? Why did his victory look like defeat? How did he break through the fortifications?

The answer came to me in the shape of a tiny Baby, the seed from which a Kingdom would spring. Like a shoot on a dead branch, it was so small that it wouldn't activate the mines all around me, so insignificant that the guards wouldn't notice it slipping beneath the barbed wire, and so helpless that it was hardly worth bothering to kill. "Seek for the same helpless insignificance in yourself," the Child seemed to say. "Let that be your key to freedom."

To take this total reversal of my flawed human logic on board was going to require a revolution. But revolution is a real possibility, and miracles can be prayed for and expected.

SUGGESTIONS FOR PRAYER AND REFLECTION 3

Yahweh says this:
"A curse on the man who puts his trust in man,
who relies on things of flesh,
whose heart turns from Yahweh.
He is like dry scrub in the wastelands:
if good comes, he has no eyes for it,
he settles in the parched places of the wilderness,
a salt land, uninhabited."

"A blessing on the man who puts his trust in Yahweh,
with Yahweh for his hope.
He is like a tree by the waterside

that thrusts its roots to the stream:

when the heat comes it feels no alarm,

its foliage stays green;

it has no worries in a year of drought,

and never ceases to bear fruit."   (Jeremiah 17:5–8)

READ THESE WORDS, slowly and peacefully, and reread them again and again for as long as you feel drawn to stay with them. In your imagination, picture the two trees that Jeremiah speaks of: the "dry scrub in the wastelands" and the "tree by the waterside that thrusts its roots to the stream."

Let yourself enter, imaginatively, into the life of the first tree, the "dry scrub." Try to feel its thirst, its brittleness, its sense of being disconnected from the source of its being. Feel the burning heat of the desert. Taste the corrosive saltiness of the dry air. Feel the stinging in your eyes, blinding you to the world around you. Imagine the gradual dying away of all your life energy, until you sink into the sand and are forgotten.

Now try to enter into the life of the second tree, which grows at the waterside. Feel your roots going deep into the cool earth and finding the life-sustaining water. Notice the cover of green foliage, shielding you from the burning sun. Enjoy the taste of fruit growing on your boughs. Relax in the certainty that no drought can destroy you because your roots are connected to the groundwater.

Bring your feelings about the two trees to God in your prayer, perhaps expressing your distress at those aspects of your being that are disconnected from him, and your joy at those things in you that are rooted in your trust of him.

LOOK BACK OVER the events of the last twenty-four hours. Notice just one special moment, or event, or encounter that has given you joy and helped you to remember that you are loved. Look back over your life's journey, remembering those milestones that seem, with hindsight, truly to have made your life worthwhile. Remember one special person who has made you aware of God's unconditional love for you, perhaps by giving you their own. Offer God your gratitude for these repeated signs of his love for you, and ask him for the grace to trust in that love when you are feeling hurt and broken.

IMAGINE YOURSELF AS A wounded bird savaged by a cat, or as an animal caught in a trap, or as a small child who has hurt herself because she disobeyed her parents' instructions. Now, without offering any excuses or justifications or reproaches against what has harmed you, just let yourself be gathered up by God and held gently in the palm of his hand. Be still, and simply know that he is God, who loves you and desires your wholeness so much that he is ready to die for it.

IS THERE A SITUATION in your life that feels like the "lock chamber," where you feel trapped, and where all your efforts and desires seem quite meaningless, and there seems to be no way out? You might like to lay this situation before God in your prayer and ask him to show you any ways in which it has meaning and significance beyond the results (or lack of them) that you are able to see. For example, you may spend all your days in a job that seems to benefit no one and makes you frustrated. Let your job unfold in your prayer, and ask God to change your perspective, to see any ways in which it makes a difference whether you do your work with joy or with resistance. If you feel able to do so, try to make a real human contact with a colleague or another person who is trapped in a similar situation, and listen to their feelings about where they find themselves. If you can do this, then however pointless your work may seem, it will have become a place where true human communion has become possible.

GOD IS IN ALL things and therefore God is in the "lock chamber." Try placing some symbol of your faith in the place where you feel trapped, for example, in the office, in the kitchen, or in the car. This could be a candle or a flower, an icon, or some small thing that is significant only to yourself. Let this become a constant reminder to you that this place of your apparent imprisonment is sacred space because God is there. Similarly, try taking five minutes every so often during the day to be

> The gospel is about the power of God coming to us in a helpless refugee baby and a condemned and executed man. At what turning points in your life did you know that God's power was active in you when you felt most helpless or inadequate? Recall one of these times in prayer, and take this awareness into your heart: "God's power is seen most surely in our weakness."

away from your work, perhaps just by taking a short walk in the garden or down the corridor or around the car parking lot, or even to the coffee machine and back. Be deliberate about taking this time just for yourself alone, but, equally deliberately, ask God to walk with you. Don't try to make it a time of elaborate prayer. Just let it be time when you remember consciously that you and God are in this thing together. In this way, your five minutes will be sacred, and the whole day will be touched by this sacred time, as the Sabbath touches the whole week into sacredness.

CAN YOU NAME any of the "signposts" that have pointed you toward God as your life has unfolded? Now, in the honesty of your own heart, do you notice any points when you have stayed with the signposts instead of walking on beyond them? For example, you may have become fixed on a particular kind of liturgy and feel bereft if you can't find a church that is on your wavelength, or you may be becoming trapped in a compulsive need to pray in a particular way, at a particular time, or in a special place, and feel disturbed if anything interferes with this. If you find any long-term settlements like this, just ask God to help you see beyond them to where he is beckoning you forward. But be gentle with yourself.

WE HAVE ALMOST all been brought up to value our independence. What aspects of your independence do you especially cherish? Now make a list of all the things that your "independence" depends on—a car, for example, or the maintenance of your good health, the availability of child care, a reliable kennel to look after your pet while you are on retreat, uninterrupted gas and water supplies, an understanding doctor, a job that doesn't require you to work on Sundays, a word processor that corrects your spelling, a refrigerator that saves you from having to go to the grocery store every day, a wife who remembers where you left your glasses.

These are just a few examples of the very many things we take for granted in our assumptions about independence. I remember especially the day I dropped my driving glasses on the doorstep and realized how the most trivial accident like this was able to immobilize me and to rob me of my much cherished vision! It also made me realize how heavily I depend on my emergency services, like a willing and competent optician, and on the money needed to pay for them in my hour of need.

4

LETTING GOD BE GOD

TRANSFORMATION IS going to involve a revolution! In this chapter we look at what happens when we make the earth-shattering discovery, like Copernicus before us, that the sun does not revolve around the earth but that the earth revolves around the sun or, in more personal language, that neither God nor his creation revolves around *us,* but we and all creation revolve around, and are centered in, God.

At this point in our growth path toward our deepest eternal reality, we have to make a radical switch of focus. God challenges us to cease to be self-centered, that is, in orbit around our own kingdoms, and to become God-centered. This is an uncomfortable moment. More probably, for most of us, it is an ongoing discomfort that never goes away throughout our adult lives. Once we have become aware of the way things really are organized, we can never again be quite comfortable with ourselves when we are living as though things were still the way our illusions had seduced us into believing.

A simple experiment is sometimes used to bring this reality vividly alive. Stand with a light source behind you, and walk steadily away from the light source. Notice where your shadow falls. And notice whether the path ahead seems dark or well lit. Now turn to face the light source. What happens to your shadow? How does the path ahead of you look now?

Something similar happens on our inner journey. When we are oriented toward our own kingdoms, and away from the sun, our God center, where does the shadow fall? How does it leave us feeling? What do we have to do to change things? In fact, all we need to do is to turn around. There is no requirement to walk all the way back, retracing the wrong pathways in reverse. As soon as we make the radical shift of focus, we automatically expose ourselves to the sun's rays. What does that do to the shadow?

On a smaller scale, I remember, as a child, being mystified when my parents used to complain that I was sitting in my own light as I sat reading or doing my homework with my back to the window or to the lamp. At the time, I thought it was just another way the grown-ups had devised to interfere with my freedom and find fault with my way of doing things, and I often stubbornly refused to turn around and enjoy the full stream of light on my work. Of course, if I did do the sensible thing, it made a big difference to my ability to discern things . . . reluctant though I might have been to admit it!

Now, on reflection, the words "sitting in my own light" leap off the paper and hit me between the eyes. What a description of fallenness! Here we sit, basking in our own light (rather than in God's), so sure of its continuance and its glory, while all the time we are actually casting our own shadow over everything and everyone in our line of vision.

There are two major problems with this position.

The first is that, like the earth, we don't have such a thing as "our own light." That's not how things are. The light that may seem to illuminate us is not ours at all, but the reflected light of the sun and, ultimately, of God. This is a fundamental difference between the Creator and the creature. Recognizing our creaturehood is probably the most painful part of the Copernican revolution. It means letting go of that certainty that we are somehow the source, or at least the controller, of our own being.

The second problem is the matter of the shadow. If I remain with my back to the light source or, rather, to God, who is the source of my being, my own bulk (which is just an image for my ego) will overshadow all

> Sin is not just a shopping list of misdemeanors to bring to the confessional. It is a radical inside-outness, and the more we try to sort it out for ourselves, the more entangled we will become.

that I do—all my efforts, all my relationships, all my journey. Not only will I not be able to see the way ahead because of my own shadow, but I will cast the darkness over others. I will make the world a darker place. And, of course, the bigger my ego, the larger and darker the shadow I cast will be.

There is another subtle twist when it comes to deluding ourselves that we are suns rather than planets. Having convinced ourselves that we are our own light and our own center of gravity, the next step is not far behind, when we begin to think that other beings should revolve around us. In this way, we can set up whole systems or hierarchies of fallenness, and the shadow of sin looms ever larger and more darkly over life on earth. We who were created, as Ignatius says, "to praise, reverence, and serve God," begin to spend our energies trying to arrange that others and, indeed, that all of creation, should exist to praise, reverence, and serve us.

To see this dynamic in action, it's usually easier to watch it happening to us rather than because of us. Perhaps you are aware of situations or relationships where you feel that, though you are not centered on God, you are not entirely centered on yourself either. It may well be, then, that you are being drawn into orbit around someone else's (false) center and are in their magnetic field, so to speak. This may be through your own choice or through their manipulative influence (deliberate or unconscious) upon you. Either way, it is not helping you to draw closer to God; rather, it is impeding your journey and undermining your inner freedom and may need to be prayerfully examined and resisted.

If we recognize God as our sun, that is, as the source and upholder of all our being, and ourselves as planets whose natural movement is to be in orbit around our Source, then we can come closer to the real meaning of two words that are used by masters of the spiritual life, including Ignatius. These words are *consolation* and *desolation*—words that carry a rather different meaning in the context of our inner journey from the meanings we associate with them in everyday speech.

What do we mean when we talk of consolation and desolation? We are really only talking about our orientation, and the bottom line is this: which direction is our life taking us—toward God or away from him? Turning, or *metanoia*, can sound like a sudden dramatic conversion exercise, and for some people it may come as a onetime Damascus experience. But for most it is a gradual process that extends through life. And even for the Damascus people, the experience continues in every lived moment, in every choice we make, however apparently trivial. Every moment of our lives is a moment in which we can be toward the sun or away from it; we can be moving toward consolation or drifting into desolation.

How do we tell the difference? And what can we do about it? Before we go on to reflect more deeply (in later chapters) on the movements of our moods, we need first to get in touch with Ignatius's understanding of how our moods will reflect a different underlying pattern depending on whether the general direction of our lives is toward God or away from him. To allay any dismay at this point, it is important to stress that those who are reading a book like this and are seeking to deepen their prayer, are almost certainly not, in a general way, moving away from God. We may, however, all too easily find ourselves temporarily drifting away from our desired destination, and many of us will recall times in our lives when this state of things was more lasting and ingrained.

Ignatius explains the underlying patterns of the moods of the two orientations (toward or away from God) like this:

- For those drifting away from God, the action of God in their lives disturbs them and churns up their moods, creating peacelessness, while the things that come from their own kingdoms make them feel good and leave them apparently contented.

- For those whose lives are moving toward God, the opposite effects are apparent: when God is touching them, they feel at peace and they know that somehow they are on solid ground; when they are (hopefully temporarily) attending to their own kingdoms, they feel that they are not really living true, and they experience inner turmoil.

Another way of looking at the effects of our inner movements is through the example of the tide ebbing and flowing onto a beach. If we imagine that the beach represents our true center and home in God, and the destination of our journeying, we can see that the sea is either moving toward the beach (flow tide) or away from it (ebb tide). In the same way, our hearts, our truest centers, are directed either toward or away from God. This represents the general orientation of our lives. Now look at the effect of the winds, which we might compare to the action of what Ignatius calls "the spirits." Imagine the effect on a swimmer who is moving, in general terms, with the tidal flow, when the wind is blowing against the direction of the tide: If the wind is blowing out to sea, then it will impede the progress of the person swimming with the flow tide by working in the opposite direction; If the wind is blowing in from offshore, it will accelerate the swimmer's progress. The opposite effects can be seen in the way these same winds work on a swimmer who is moving out to sea on an ebb tide.

If we translate this into the language of our spiritual journey, we can see that when we are directed toward our home in God, a wind in the opposite direction will cause turbulence and act obstructively. Yet the same wind would be perceived as a benefit to those whose journey is directed away from God. If we now acknowledge that these winds represent the creative and destructive spirits, or movements, working in our hearts, we can begin to understand how a spirit, or an inner movement that speeds and affirms the journey of a pilgrim on his way toward God would appear as a movement of opposition for a person whose life is directed away from God.

Since we can assume that all of us who are joined together in the fellowship of this book, to deepen our life in God, have the same basic orientation toward God and toward our home in him (the "beach"), we can see from this example that the bad spirits are like the wind blowing against us and making us feel that we are up against blocks and obstructions, and experiencing turbulence and distress, while the good spirits are like the wind blowing from behind us, giving us a sense of support and encouragement and apparently speeding our journey and cooperating with it.

Of course these are only metaphors. Not everyone today would readily identify with Ignatius's notion of the spirits as separate, objectively real entities, sent either to try us or to cheer us. Yet all of us know that we experience these different movements in our hearts. Sometimes they clearly spring from our own inner lives, our moods, and our intentions. Sometimes they appear to beset us from outside, for no apparent reason, and very occasionally we may experience a real sense of being at the mercy of evil forces beyond our human comprehension. Our aim here is not to try to identify the various ways in which negative or positive inner movements arise, but rather to understand their effects so that we can become better able to respond to them. We do this by welcoming and giving thanks for the times of consolation, when the winds are with us, and by being on guard when we encounter the movements of desolation when the winds are against us.

A Crisis in the Tunnel?

Ignatius gives us an absolute rule for handling desolation:

> When in desolation, don't make life-changing decisions, and don't go back on a decision that you took during a period of consolation.

If you translate this into the language of the tides and the winds, it would be equivalent to sensing an opposing wind when you are swimming to shore on a flow-tide, and because you meet the opposition of the wind and experience the turbulence, you decide to turn around and let the wind blow you back out to sea. How many of us have had such an experience, when circumstances turned against us and our response was something like, "I always knew it was pointless; I don't know what possessed me to try. I'm quitting."

A friend of mine, who has given permission for her story to be shared, recently suffered a tragic bereavement that left her shocked and stunned for many months. A few months after this loss, she and her husband had a holiday together on a canal narrow boat, and afterwards she shared her thoughts on how it felt to be traveling through a tunnel.

To enter the tunnel, she said, was like entering a dark night, such as the one she had just experienced in the loss of her friend. Even the slightest bends in the length of the tunnel mean that the light from the exit is obscured. In a tunnel you can lose all sense of perspective; you can almost forget that there ever was daylight. This is how she describes it:

"You cannot see even your hand in front of you without a light to guide you. The exit is not visible as you go through the tunnel; you have to trust that it is there once you have entered the tunnel's mouth. It is an unpleasant experience because of the difficulties encountered along the way—narrowly missing other boats, scraping or bumping into the walls, the smells, the dark, the diesel fumes that hang in the air and choke you...."

This is a vivid picture of how spiritual desolation can feel, though of course each person's experience is unique. Small wonder that in such inner circumstances we are tempted to give up, turn back, change direction, and reverse the decision we first made to make the journey that has led us into this tunnel. It was at this point in her reflection that my friend made her own discovery of Ignatius's wisdom:

"You can't turn a forty-foot boat round in a tunnel, so once you have started you have to continue. To reverse is to lose your steering control."

This picture is one of the most vivid images I have ever encountered of the reality of Ignatius's warning about not changing course during a period of desolation. It bears prayerful reflection:

- If you try to turn a forty-foot boat around in a tunnel, you will cause a thoroughgoing shipwreck. Your life, and your journey with God, are on board that boat. Don't risk sinking them forever in the depths of that dark tunnel.

- Nor is backpedaling a realistic alternative: it doesn't work, because it robs you of your steering control. Difficult enough to reverse safely in a car, but try walking backwards in a straight line with your eyes closed for any distance. At best you may get back to where you began, albeit with bumps and scars and gashes from your blind collisions on the reverse journey. But is that really where you want to be—back where you began?

And so my friend realized, out of her own deeply felt dark night experience, that the tunnel was indeed the only way to move onward toward the desired destination, and that all tunnels, however dark, do come to an end. The reality of the journey is not the tunnel but the canal, not the period of dark desolation, but the reality of God's light forever shining, even when we do not see it. She concludes her story:

"When you emerge on the other side, the light seems brighter, the birdsong sweeter and the dappling in the water more beautiful. You see the world with new eyes because of the darkness behind you. You have arrived at a new place further on in your journey."

In the next chapter we will look more deeply into the question of how to recognize our moods of consolation and desolation and where their roots might be located.

Meanwhile, we might reflect on the question, Whose kingdom am I really serving—my own or God's? And while we might be able to answer that question positively, acknowledging God's kingship in a general way, how does it look when we reflect honestly over the particular details of, say, the past twenty-four hours? A deeper look at our changing moods and reactions may tell another story.

SUGGESTIONS FOR PRAYER AND REFLECTION 4

May Yahweh bless you and keep you.

May Yahweh let his face shine on you and be gracious to you.

May Yahweh uncover his face to you

and bring you peace.   (Numbers 6:24–26)

READ THIS TEXT slowly and prayerfully, letting its meanings and its resonances soak deeply into your heart. Read it over and over, as a cow chews its cud, slowly extracting its special flavor and absorbing its nourishment into your Who center, to feed the roots of the Who you are becoming.

If any phrase or word especially attracts you, stay with it and repeat it to yourself, savoring it and letting God be in it for you.

Allow yourself simply to *be,* in stillness of heart and mind, before God, whose face is shining upon you, warming you into eternal life. Be present to him, as he is to you, simply absorbing his love and his grace. Relax into his depths and let him open up your own depths to the coming of his springtime.

HAS THERE BEEN a time in your life when you were consistently drifting away from God, either by accident or deliberately? Recall that time now in prayer, and offer it to God for his healing and forgiveness.

REMEMBER THE CIRCUMSTANCES in which you changed direction, maybe suddenly, maybe gradually. Remember where you were living, what you were doing, how old you were at the time. Recall any other human companions who played a part in helping you to turn back to God. Remember and express your gratitude to God.

LOOK BACK OVER the past twenty-four hours. Did you experience any contra winds during that time? Any following winds? How did they make you feel?

Can you recall a time when you made a decision to do something when you were in consolation, but then reversed that decision when the winds started to blow against you? Can you recall a time when you stayed with a decision made in consolation, even though you came up against the contra winds of desolation and turmoil? Now compare your feelings about those two situations.

REFLECT ON THE QUESTION, Whose kingdom am I really serving? My own kingdom? Another person's kingdom? God's kingdom? Apply it to the specific events of the past day or week.

To decide whose kingdom is being served by a particular course of action, it is helpful to open up the real motives for what is being done, and to do this with complete honesty before God in prayer. As an example, we might hear a politician declaring that he is taking a controversial course of action because it is "in the national interest," but if we look more deeply, we can see that the main motivator is the forthcoming election or the need to save face at tomorrow's cabinet meeting.

Warning: It is very easy to answer the question for other people's actions and decisions! It is far from easy to exercise the same degree of honesty in ourselves! To do so, we need God and prayer and humility (and a sense of humor!).

5

TRACKING OUR MOODS

W E ALL KNOW that we are subject to moods that appear to change unpredictably and often uncontrollably. In the last chapter we noticed that there is a fundamental difference between the feelings we sometimes experience of "being on solid ground," or of "living true," and the opposite feelings of being "at odds with ourselves" and in a state of inner turmoil. In this chapter we will try to discover the underlying patterns of these moods and what they can show us of our journey with God.

As we noticed in the last chapter, it is taken as a fact of our lives that our basic orientation is toward God; otherwise we would not be seeking to deepen our lives with him in this way. It follows, then, that when we experience the "solid" feelings, these are springing, however remotely, from God's action upon us. When we experience feelings of turmoil, these will have their ultimate source in something that is not of God but has to do with our own kingdoms.

Tracing the Moods of the Day

To get in touch with the changing moods of your lived experience, try this exercise: first, steady and still yourself until you feel that you are in your Who center. Now look back over the last twenty-four hours, or possibly over a longer period, perhaps a week or even a year. Simply replay the time under review prayerfully, and allow the dominant moods of that period to surface again. It may be helpful to make a note (at least mentally, perhaps written down) of when in the review period you touched on solid feelings (we could call these "rosebed" reactions) and when you touched on turmoil (we could call these "nettlebed" reactions). Undoubtedly both kinds of feelings will have been present, to some degree in any period of time, and there is no reason to feel guilty about this.

The next stage is to allow God, in the prayer, to lead us down to the real roots of those feelings and those moods. If I felt a surge of rage about something, or a wave of fear or apprehension, what prompted it? Someone stepped on one of my cherished dreams, perhaps, or offended my pride, or bumped into some "furniture" in my secret inner room. If that happened, where exactly was the sore spot located, and does it remind me of other times when the same sore spot has been touched on? What is that sore spot really about? Can we put a name to it and own it?

Now let's look at those moments when we were on solid ground. What was the trigger for those feelings? What was I doing at the time? Whom was I with? What was said or done to kindle the good feeling? Perhaps it was a moment in touch with God's creation, and I felt my own deep connection to it. Perhaps it was a moment of insight, when I felt that God had given me a flash of understanding about myself, a situation, or a relationship. Perhaps I was touched unexpectedly by the kindness and love of another, or my own feelings of love and compassion were triggered by the needs of someone else. Where was that point of stillness and peace located? Does it remind me of other similar moments in my experience? Where is its real source, and what new growth does it lead to? Just as with the sore spots, we can name the good times and own them. They are ours — a gift from God.

For example, "nettlebed" feelings of depression may be rooted in anxieties about the future; feelings of distrust may spring from a broken relationship; feelings of cynicism may be rooted in an earlier betrayal of friendship; violent reactions may be coming from the experience of abuse in childhood; and attitudes of arrogance frequently stem from past humiliations.

"Rosebed" reactions of confidence may be rooted in experiences of affirmation; joy may be coming from yesterday's sunset; compassion may be growing out of the experience of being understood by friends; tolerance flows from the experience of being forgiven; and the possibility of being loving comes from the experience of being loved.

The exercise just described is commonly called a "review of consciousness" prayer. Ignatius urged his companions to make a review of consciousness every day, even if they had no time for any other form of prayer. In this way, he taught them how to track their own moods and discover the deeper movements in their hearts, learning to recognize the solid-ground moods as consolation and the moods of inner turmoil as desolation. Over time, this practice will help us to see where the deepest desires of our hearts really lie, and it will reveal where our deepest unease is located. It will also help us to distinguish between the movements of God within us, which result in consolation, and the movements that spring from our own kingdoms or from the pressure of other people's kingdoms, which tend toward desolation.

Noticing Our Inner Furniture

The furniture in our inner rooms makes us particularly accident prone, and it has the major disadvantage of being invisible to those unfortunates who may crash into it without warning. It is likely to be invisible to ourselves as well, unless and until we let God reveal it to us in our prayer and reflection on what is happening in our lives. We all have this kind of furniture, which may have to do with bad memories and experiences or some irrational prejudice that has its roots in our own histories.

Imagine a young mother who is happy to show off her new baby. Despite wanting to convey support and admiration, her friend is suddenly brought up against the raw memories of a lost, or perhaps aborted, child, memories she thought she had dealt with but are actually waiting to surface at the slightest opportunity. The joy of the one person and the grief of the other are on a collision course, and neither may understand the reasons for the tension that is brewing between them.

The trick with the inner furniture is not to try to get rid of it. No one can do that; we are all inhabited by our memories and our fears. We do, however, want to make it visible to ourselves. Once we know that it is there, and what it looks like, people will still bump into it, but we will have moved beyond the risk of being thrown off course by those bumps. That makes us more free, and it also creates a free space for others, who no longer experience the tension of our hidden "Don't touch!" notices.

- When you have recognized and acknowledged an item of your own inner furniture, you will not be thrown when someone bumps into it.
- This will make you more free.
- It will also create a free space for others, who will realize, subconsciously, that this issue is no longer a keep-out area, and they will feel inwardly safe in opening it up with you.

Some Bomb-Disposal Techniques

My own inner furniture suffered some bruising one evening, as I well remember, during a discussion on Thomas Merton. This spiritual giant, whom I much admire, was also a vowed religious who broke the spirit of his vows in later life when he fell in love. Something in this incongruity struck a raw nerve in me that I didn't realize was there. In no time at all, the discussion became disordered and unproductive as I, and others, groped around in the inner darkness of our mixed reactions, trying to put our furniture back to rights. My own overreaction so troubled me that I shared it with a spiritual director, who helped me to get to the root of my own disturbance about the subject, and also to realize that my reaction had a good deal more to do with me than with Thomas Merton.

It happened, however, that only a few weeks later, someone spoke with me about a personal dilemma that also had strong connections with "the Thomas Merton affair." Though I wasn't conscious of it at the time, I realized afterward that while listening to this person's story, I had not experienced any inner turmoil of my own but had been able to give my undivided attention. This would not have been possible if I hadn't been through the experience in the discussion group. As it was, I had already encountered this particular piece of inner furniture and was no longer thrown by someone's bumping into it again.

If you find it difficult to imagine the difference between safe and un-safe space in another person's response to you, perhaps you have met one of those prickly people who seem always to need handling with great care. These are the sort of people with whom you find yourself thinking, or even saying to yourself (and your children!), "Whatever you do, don't mention such and such." The taboo subjects can grow into a long list with some people — most of us have come across them! Now take your thoughts one step further and notice how you react to such people. I suggest that you will discover that you are very wary about what you talk about with them, and in extreme cases, you may start to avoid them altogether because they seem to be surrounded by a ring of invisible barbed wire.

All this tends to happen at a level below normal everyday awareness. One way into it is to notice your own overreactions. These may well be pointing, as they were with me, to an area of tension inside you. If you can get in touch with the roots of this tension, possibly with the help of an understanding friend, you will go a long way toward defusing it. And others may have reason to be very grateful for your land-mine-clearance operation, because it will increase the safe space within you, where they may now safely venture.

Consolation and Desolation — How to Recognize Them

Most of our feelings of desolation and consolation can be traced back to the kinds of roots we have been looking at in this chapter, but how do they show themselves in practice? Here are some of the main symptoms of desolation and the most commonly experienced blessings of conso-lation.

Desolation

- turns us in on ourselves
- drives us down the spiral ever deeper into our own negative feelings
- cuts us off from community

- makes us want to give up on the things that used to be important to us
- takes over our whole consciousness and crowds out our distant vision
- covers up all our landmarks
- drains us of energy

Consolation
- directs our focus outside and beyond ourselves
- lifts our hearts so that we can see the joys and sorrows of other people
- bonds us more closely to our human community
- generates new inspiration and ideas
- restores balance and refreshes our inner vision
- shows us where God is active in our lives and where he is leading us
- releases new energy in us

You may find it helpful to look back again over the moods of the past twenty-four hours and see whether you recognize any of these symptoms or have experienced any of these blessings.

In whatever ways we ourselves have experienced consolation and have felt ourselves, however briefly, to be close to God, these are moments to thank him for wholeheartedly, and moments to cherish in memory and return to deliberately when we find ourselves in periods of desolation, as a child returns to its parent's arms when things get difficult and bewildering in the outside world. To help us remember, it is good to write down our feelings at times of consolation and keep our memories accessible in this way.

Consolation is not the same as happiness. It is possible to be in consolation, and very close to God, at times of real objective pain. I personally remember the two or three weeks of vigil as my mother was dying of cancer as a time of unusual closeness to God. Similarly, consolation can often give rise to tears. There is a big difference between tears of consolation and tears of desolation. Take a moment to recall how it feels when you have wept tears of desolation, winding yourself down ever more deeply into despair, and when you have felt so overwhelmed with joy, or with a sense of the presence of God, that your heart has filled up and overflowed in inexplicable tears, which were the tears of consolation.

Another useful test to apply to our moods is this: in a particular situation, am I feeling drawn, powerfully perhaps but always gently, or am I feeling driven? To get in touch with the difference between these feelings, we can recall times when someone has asked us to do something, and reflect on our response. Did we say yes because we felt we really, deep down, wanted to do it, or did we go along with it to please someone else or to avoid conflict, but against our deeper inclinations? The action of God on our lives is always, at its heart, experienced as a drawing. If we are feeling driven, then the prompting that gives rise to it is not from God but from the force fields of our own (or other people's) kingdoms. Ignatius compares consolation to the action of water falling softly onto a sponge, and desolation to the action of water splashing onto stone.

When I find my heart shrinking and sinking and turning to lead, I often repeat to myself, like a mantra, the words, "Lift up your hearts: we lift them to the Lord!" You may like to find some phrase or image that helps you at times like these to check the downward spiral of desolation. My daughter has given me a visual aid for this exercise—a little red wooden heart that tilts up and down at the end of a green stick. It sits next to my alarm clock and helps me remember Who has given me the new day that I feel inclined to complain about!

The feelings and moods of the day that we have been tracking are about the kinds of consolation and desolation that we all experience in every day that we live. Sometimes, however, a wave of consolation seems to sweep over us for no apparent reason. It comes as a gratuitous gift from God (like all consolation), but it has the power to bowl us over. There are moments like these in Scripture, especially in the Gospels and in Acts. And we may be able to see the presence of such encounters in our own lives. Ignatius calls this experience consolation without previous cause because it has no apparent trigger. Such an experience can only be received and welcomed in all humility. Often it seems to be given not to the most deserving but to the most needy and the most unlikely recipients. It can never be achieved and should not be looked for. Those who know such an experience often say, with hindsight, that it appears to have come just before a very difficult and challenging time in their lives, seemingly as a preparation and a strengthening for what lay ahead.

Consolation and the "Feel-Good Factor"

It isn't always obvious that there is a difference between experiencing spiritual consolation and simply feeling good, or between finding oneself in spiritual desolation and simply feeling low. The effects can be very similar, but in fact the source is quite different.

To understand this fundamental difference, we really do need to notice the *direction of our attention* as we go through the experience. The feel-good factor, as cultivated by politicians in particular, and its counterpart of feeling low, is intrinsically focused on ourselves. Things happen in our own kingdoms that trigger these ups and downs. In national terms, a reduction in taxation, for example, is supposed to lift our hearts. At home, a family row can pitch us into the depths. If we could see the way our feelings are directed, we would notice that they are pointing in toward ourselves and the satisfaction or disruption of our own personal worlds. This is completely natural, of course, and it is part of what makes us human. However, it can very easily, as we know, be deliberately manipulated, or affected by such things as our changing body chemistry or how well we slept last night. These swings are not at all the same thing as spiritual consolation or desolation.

And the difference seems to lie in the focus of the experience. Spiritual consolation is experienced when our hearts are drawn toward God, even if, as we have seen, this happens in circumstances that the world would regard as negative. It is a signal that our hearts, at least for that moment, are beating in harmony with the heart of God. Consolation is the experience of this deep connectedness to God, and it fills our being with a sense of peace and joy. The epicenter of the experience lies in God and not in ourselves.

The reverse is true of spiritual desolation. This is felt when our hearts are turned away from God. A common pattern of desolation might look like this:

- Something happens in my life that upsets my kingdom. Perhaps a desire of mine is frustrated, or something wounding is said or done to me.

- I react to the event by focusing on my own pain. This has the effect of turning my attention away from God and onto myself.

- I then find myself, as it were, standing with my back to the light and seeing only my own shadow. As a result, the world appears dark and threatening.

- I can then all too easily imagine worse and worse consequences of the original negative event, and so I spiral down into deeper and deeper layers of desolation.

If we can learn to recognize these patterns, we can turn the negative movement around. The same unpleasant event may occur, but we can choose to react to it by trying to focus outward, Godward, instead of inward upon our own pain. (This is by no means easy and is possible only if our deep desire to move closer to God is actually stronger than the feeling of pain the event has caused in us. We will look more closely at this problem in a later chapter.)

When this begins to happen, we may experience a real breakthrough, leading to the discovery that God is actually drawing us closer to him through the very event that appears (at the Where level of ourselves) to be so destructive.

This turning, or refocusing, is a kind of ongoing, day-by-day, hour-by-hour conversion. Such turnings are often invisible to anyone but ourselves and God, yet they can be more costly, more truly authentic, and more likely to lead toward lasting change than the more dramatic Damascus experiences. Every day of our lives will bring its own share of little dyings, and in this sense we are called to a rebirth every time we react by turning toward God instead of in upon ourselves. To be born again is truly a continuous process.

> Consolation and desolation are infectious, and yet, strangely, the best advice is not to keep them to yourself!

One last word about consolation and desolation before we move to the next chapter to consider ways of using our moods to help us find our way in the dark. Our moods, as we know to our cost, are highly infectious. How often have we clouded the hearts of our whole family or community by infecting them with our desolation, and how often have we felt ourselves being drawn down the deadly spiral of another person's desolation? On the other hand, the next time you are driving to town on a sunny morning, notice how many of your fellow drivers are smiling, or are singing to the car radio, or are eager to acknowledge your courtesy if you give them the right of way! And notice what that does to your own mood.

Desolation will choke you, so give your feelings over to God (not as easy as it sounds, but keep doing it anyway!) and turn your attention away from yourself and toward other people. Consolation will make you want to overflow with joy, so share your feelings with others, let the energy that consolation generates fuel your dreams and visions, and say thank you to God.

You might like to end this chapter by staying, in prayer, with a specific moment or period of consolation that you recall and asking God to show you how to respond to it in a way that makes it a seed of growth for yourself and for others.

SUGGESTIONS FOR PRAYER AND REFLECTION 5

TRY REFLECTING BACK over the past twenty-four hours (or a longer period if you wish), using the "review of consciousness" prayer. The guidelines in *My Day with God: An Evening Prayer,* on pages 59–61 may help you to notice where God has been present to you in the events and encounters of the day.

IN STILLNESS, TAKE the time to notice especially the moods of this past day. Have you experienced "nettlebed" feelings at all? If so, can you trace their roots? What was really at the heart of the hurting? Have you spent any time in the rose garden? Remember those moments, and thank God for them. Then try to notice where they had their roots. Let your gratitude for those nourishing roots come to the surface. Thank God for them, and remember in your prayer any people, dead or alive, who have nourished your good roots.

TAKE TIME TO LOOK inside your "inner rooms." Is there any "furniture" standing there? Are there any "Don't touch!" notices? Has anybody bumped into your furniture recently? How did it feel? Did it surprise you? What did it reveal to you about your invisible furniture? Have you bumped into anyone else's furniture?

Have people infected you with their desolation today? Or their consolation? How did you react to it? How did it leave you feeling? Do you think that you yourself infected anyone else, either with desolation or consolation?

REFLECT ON ANY situation in your life where you are feeling driven. Who or what is doing the driving? Do you want it to be like that? If the situation troubles you, bring it to God now in prayer, and show him how you are feeling. Let him lead you gently toward an understanding of the forces that are driving you, and where they have their source. Ask him to free you from any repeating patterns of drivenness that you are experiencing.

Now reflect on those aspects of your life where you feel you are being drawn. How do they feel? Peaceful? Challenging? Exciting? Frightening? Try to describe them to yourself. Bring them to God in your prayer, and let him show you where these things have their source. Let him affirm and strengthen those responses and feelings in you that have their origins in his guiding of your life.

CHOOSE A PHRASE, or mantra, or an image for yourself that you feel would help you when you find yourself spiraling down into desolation.

This may be a phrase from Scripture or from a favorite book or poem, or an endearment, or a name for God, a warm memory, or a much loved scene. Whatever you choose, store it away for yourself for a rainy day.

My Day with God: An Evening Prayer

The day is drawing to a close. Work, family, chores, children, life itself have filled every moment. Or perhaps the day was empty, long, and lonely. There may have been no time or inclination for prayer, but there has been plenty of time and space for God.

Where was he? How was he?

This prayerful reflection, which can be made in as little as ten minutes, has been used for centuries by countless believers. It can help to draw your day together and open your eyes to the intricate and beautiful patterns of light, shade, and color that the Lord has been weaving through the fabric of your minutes and your hours.

The pattern of the prayer is like this:

STILLNESS. Relax; be still; let the tensions of the day slip away from you. Know that you are in God's presence. He rejoices that you have come to him, however forgetful you may have been of him during the day.

THANKFULNESS. Remember with thanksgiving the gifts of God to you today. A meeting with a friend; a glimpse of deep joy or sadness in a passing face; a flower at the wayside; a baby's first steps; a grandparent's smile; a friendly shop assistant; a considerate driver; a moment of insight; a job done; a problem solved; a child's hug; a lover's touch; a warm memory; a rising moon; a falling leaf. . . . Be still in the memory, and offer God your thanks in your own way.

LIGHT-SEEKING. Ask God to help you see and understand how his love has been working within you today. This is a gift of the Spirit, and it has been promised to all who sincerely seek it.

REFLECTION. Reflect peacefully on what has been happening to you and in you today, trusting that your prayer for the light of his Spirit has been granted. Let him show you whatever he may want to show you. The questions that follow are only suggestions to prompt your reflection. If you feel drawn to a particular question, stay with it, and let God speak to your heart about it:

- How were you drawn to God today: by a friend, the beauty of nature, a book, a letter, or a gentle thought?
- Have you learned anything today about God and his ways in the everyday events of living and in the world around you?
- Did you meet him in fears, joys, work, misunderstandings, weariness, pain? (One way of meeting God is to recognize our need for him.)
- Did his word come alive for you in prayer, in Scripture, in liturgy, in his creation?
- Did you bring Christ to those around you? Did they bring him to you?
- Have you been a sign of God's presence and love to the people you met today? Did you come across someone who was lonely, sad, discouraged or in need; did you recognize the need in their eyes; did you respond?
- Did you sense the presence of God in the wider world, perhaps in what you saw on TV or read in the papers? Can you bring him your feelings—your anger, your compassion?
- Did anything happen today to make you feel loved? Were you able to show love to another person today?
- Did you feel the absence of God in any part of your day? If so, why do you think that was?
- How were your moods today? What made you feel peaceful? Where did you experience unease or even turmoil? Reflect on what it was that seemed to cause you to react with these feelings, and open them up to God, for affirmation or for healing.
- Did you feel God calling you, prompting you, nudging you in any particular way today? How did you respond?
- Out of all your day's experience, is there one special incident or discovery that you would like to thank him for?

SORROW. With hindsight you may realize that much of your reaction to the events of the day has been centered on your own kingdom. This may have led you to fail to respond to the cry of another person, or to allow your own preoccupations to take center stage and crowd out other people's needs. Your day may have left little space for an awareness of God or of his creation. Whatever inadequacies you find in your day's living, let them be there before God now, not for judgment, but for his Spirit to hover over the mess, bringing wholeness out of brokenness, as once that same Spirit brought creation out of chaos. Express your sorrow to God, and confidently ask for his healing and forgiveness.

HOPEFULNESS. Look forward to tomorrow. Ask him to open your heart to whatever surprises it may bring; to open your eyes to notice him in unexpected places; to open your ears to become tuned in to the unceasing song of his kingdom. Pray for the sensitivity to recognize the Lord in whatever ways he may greet you and call you. Something of God lies still concealed for you in tomorrow's journey. Look forward to discovering it.

Even if there is no other chance for prayer during your day, try to form the habit of reviewing your day quietly in this way each evening (or at some other appropriate time). You will quickly find that you start to look out for God's presence and his action in places you would not have thought to look before. And his promise is sure . . . those who seek him will find him.

6

Making Our Way in the Dark

W E RECALL, because it is crucially important, that because the general orientation of our lives is toward God, our feelings of consolation will point us toward his action in our lives, and our feelings of desolation will, in general, warn us that it is the things of our own kingdom that are dominating our attention.

How, then, can we use these feelings to help us find our way on the inner journey?

This chapter will look at two images that may help us: the image of the inner compass and the image of the stars.

Most of us have grown up with an uncomfortable awareness that life presents us with endless opportunities for falling into error and into sin, and we have a vague sense that some of these sins and errors are more serious in their consequences than others. Our attempts to negotiate these hurdles can feel like trying to cross a minefield. We can find ourselves thinking that if we only knew where all these mines were buried, we would know how to get to heaven without mishap. As it is, however, we spend our spiritual energy trying to hit an invisible dartboard and wonder why we get frustrated!

Of course, all this is a playful caricature, yet it has uncomfortable grains of truth. Many of us, if challenged, would find that we cherish the notion of "God's will" as something that is fixed in stone somewhere, and we believe that our task in life is to discover it and do it. The purpose of this chapter is to look at this limited understanding and see how we can get in touch with the nature of God's will more creatively and effectively, with the help of our moods and feelings. For it is there, buried in our feelings and our moods, that we can actually notice, at a real and personal level, the inner movements of our hearts and the roots of our desires and resistances, and, by grace, allow our lives to be drawn into deeper harmony with God and with our own truest center. This process then begins to look much less like aiming blindfolded at an invisible dartboard, and much more like the gradual, steady, certain evolution of a beautiful flower from its first beginnings in the seed.

But how do we find our way through the unmapped terrain of our lives and our hearts' desires and conflicts, especially when the fogs of desolation descend on us? You might like to have a look at two tools that I have found helpful in finding the way.

The Inner Compass: Where Is It and How Do I Use It?

Those of you who have done any mountain climbing will know how rapidly the clouds can come down and leave you stranded in impenetrable fog. When that happens, the guidebooks you have carefully put in your backpack become useless because you can't see any landmarks. The temptation is to try to resolve the problem by effort and activity, with the result that you go round in circles, and if you are on dangerous ground, you may well fall down a crevice or off a cliff.

A very similar thing happens to us spiritually when desolation descends on us. We lose our distant vision, and our consciousness fills up entirely with the immediate problem, whatever it is (and it may well be something that appears to be good but is actually becoming obsessive). All the useful books we have read and the sermons we have listened to lose their meaning because we can't find anything to relate them to in our immediate lived experience. And our instinctive response to all of this is to go into frantic mental activity, to "solve" the problem, or at the very least to find someone to blame for it. We quickly find ourselves going around in circles. If we are in any serious kind of trouble, there is real risk of a dangerous fall.

> To use the tool that we call *discern-ment*, we must come to stillness. In the silence of our hearts, we must wait patiently for the compass needle to steady. Then it will point to true north, the still center, the fine point of the soul, and we will be enabled to move forward again.

It is at this point that, if we are wise, on the mountains we will turn to the compass. If we know how to use it, it will show us the way, however thick the fog. To use it, we need first of all to know where it is. It needs to be readily accessible in the backpack, not twenty miles away in the youth hostel, and we need to know how to use it in conjunction with the map. Most essential, to use it, we need to stand still and let the needle come to rest.

How do these skills relate to our inner compass? They are remarkably the same, I believe. We need to know how to access our inner compass — that is, we need to be in touch with and at home with our moods, and skilled in recognizing consolation and desolation and in responding accordingly. This skill needs to be ready and primed in our hearts and not twenty miles away in our heads! We can develop this skill in prayer, with God's help, especially in the review of consciousness prayer that we looked at in the previous chapter.

Second, we need to use the compass along with the map on which the record of our experience is laid out. This map reflects our distant vision, from the times when we could see because the weather was clear. These are the times of consolation to which we must return when the clouds are down. When we place the compass on the map of our truest experience, it will reliably show us the direction we should take now that we are temporarily blinded to our destination and to the familiar landmarks.

You might use your "map," for example, to show any places and circumstances that lead you to consolation, encourage prayer, or help you become aware of your special gifts. You could also mark any habitual irritations, bad memories, fears, and resentments that tend to lead you into desolation or even despair. Notice the layout of this inner map, and become familiar with its features and contours.

Only one thing more is necessary, but it is perhaps the most difficult. We must trust the compass. How many of us hill walkers have gone through the whole procedure of taking our bearings on a fogbound summit, only to decide afterward that our own defective memories and instincts are more reliable than the compass. I have done that myself, and ended up in the wrong valley at the end of the day. I don't want to take a chance like that on my spiritual journey!

Walking by the Stars

So, the inner compass is a tool for the fogbound days, as well as being a great help when the sun shines and the way ahead seems clear and we are noticing the landmarks and signs that comprise our inner map. Another way of plotting our course is by the stars. It always fascinates me to reflect that if we could hurtle through space, we would not see any constellations. As it is, when we stand still at any point on earth beneath a clear night sky, we see these familiar patterns.

Two things are worth bearing in mind about these constellations. First, they never look quite the same from two different viewing points. Two near neighbors would see the constellations from a slightly different perspective. Two people at opposite sides of the world would see a completely different set of pictures in the heavens. Our personal view depends on where we are standing. Second, the constellations are not the reality of the stars but only the pattern we impose upon them in order to recognize them, use them to find our bearings, and talk to each other about them.

What can the constellations tell us about our inner pathfinding? I believe that when we come to stillness before God, when we let that coming-to-stillness become a habit, and when we begin to live reflectively, learning to recognize the patterns of our consolations and desolations, we begin to see the personal inner constellations of our experience that can guide us. These may be clusters of fear and anxieties to which we are particularly prone, or areas of special giftedness in our lives, ways of praying that seem consistently to bring us closer to God, aspects of our way of relating to others that tend to have destructive effects. Whether negative or positive, these personal patterns of being can be invaluable aids in steering our course in the dark. And it is significant that the stars do only shine in the dark. The dark areas of our experience can be the very places where we discover God most plainly.

As with the heavenly constellations, the patterns we discover are not the reality of ourselves but only helpful indicators of our inner movements. We might use them to locate ourselves and feel our way forward, remembering all the time that every other person's interior night sky will be different from, but no less valid than, our own.

As a practical exercise in prayer, we might ask God to lead us to the discovery of the constellations that help our journey and try to identify one cluster of gifts in ourselves, and one cluster of fears. With this knowledge in our hearts, we can use our discernment to nurture the gifts and seek freedom from the tyranny of the fears.

Staying on Course

We have some equipment for our inner journey. We have the gift of discernment, our inner compass, which will show us more and more clearly and reliably where our personal true north lies—that is, in what parts of our experience, especially our prayer experience, we are most truly centered on and directed toward God. And we have our inner constellations, which show us where our clusters of desolation and consolation are most likely to be encountered. Both these gifts are given uniquely to each individual, and each of us is personally responsible to God for developing and using them, and empowered to do so by God's indwelling Spirit at our center.

Although we are walking our own unique way with God, we are also making a journey that has been made by countless pilgrim feet before us, and Ignatius gives us some signposts on the route. These are useful whether the clouds of desolation are down and you can't see your own nose in front of you, or the sun is smiling and you can't imagine why you ever had a problem. Keep these instructions safely with your inner compass—that is, engraved on your heart! Apply the desolation rules whenever your inner compass starts to spin. Reflect on the consolation rules when your compass needle is reading true north.

And if the worst happens, and the fog gets so thick that you really can't move an inch, try using these tactics:

- Tell God, and maybe a human friend, how you feel, and ask them to pry you away from the negative force fields, even though you really want to stay where you are, in isolation.
- Force yourself to make contact with other people; go to town, walk around the market, make yourself a meal, phone a friend, even though you don't feel like doing any of these things.
- Do just one thing that needs doing (perhaps some small practical task), and then enjoy the satisfaction of having done it. Give yourself a pat on the back; then look for the next "one thing."
- Make a deliberate effort to reach out to the need of another person, maybe someone with similar difficulties, even though you really don't want to know about anyone else right now.
- Pick up a project that really fired your imagination when you were in consolation. Let it refresh you with positive energy, even though you don't actually want to do anything at all.
- Stay with the decisions you made, the dreams you dreamed when in consolation, even though you really feel like giving up on life.
- Remember moments of consolation when God seemed close to you, and reenact them in your mind, even though you are tempted to dismiss them.

If real solid desolation gets hold of you, it operates like an electric shock and literally welds you to the spot. In this situation, your concern is not for your inner progress but simply for your survival. It is likely that you won't get free of the desolating currents without help—certainly you will need God's help, and maybe that of a human friend as well, preferably one who knows what desolation can do to you. Your spiritual firefighters, in this situation, are like cutting equipment to get you free from the source of the paralysis.

You can help yourself by using the "Act against It!" method. You could compare this survival technique with what the Jesuits call *agere contra* (to act against; to drive oneself against one's inclinations). I used to think this was a perverse form of discipline that stopped your doing

What to do . . .

In Desolation:
1. Tell God how you feel and ask for help.
2. Seek out companionship.
3. Don't go back on decisions you made in consolation.
4. Stand still and remember your inner map.
5. Recall a time of consolation, and go back to it in imagination.
6. Look for someone who needs your help, and turn your attention toward them.
7. Go back to 1.

In Consolation:
1. Tell God how you feel and thank him.
2. Store this moment in your memory to return to when things get tough.
3. Add this experience to your life map.
4. Use the energy you feel to further your deepest desires.
5. Let the surplus energy fuel the things you don't like doing, and do them.
6. Go back to 1.

everything you were good at and insisted on your doing the things you were bad at, for the sake of developing humility. Now, however, I discover in my own experience that this is far from a dubious ascetic practice: it is a strategy for surviving and overcoming desolation and getting moving again on the journey home to wholeness.

And When I Go Astray?

You could be forgiven for feeling doubtful as to whether these methods are as reliable as they sound. After all, it remains a fact of our lives that, in spite of our discernment and in spite of our self-knowledge about the constellations of our lives, we can rarely look back over a day and feel that we really have been traveling true north in all our actions and decisions.

When these thoughts take hold of me, I look up to the stars and ponder the shape of the Big Dipper. When the conditions are right and the night sky is clear, I do this literally, and it has become one of my most powerful and sanity-restoring prayers.

This is the constellation that is used to locate the position of the North Star. If you start at the handle of the Big Dipper and follow it through until you reach the dipper part, and then follow the line formed by the last two stars for roughly two-and-a-half times their distance, you come to the North Star, and you are facing due north.

Try it out sometime, and relish the feeling, inwardly and outwardly, of standing facing true north with your feet planted firmly in your own backyard. This is a real promise and something to be trusted. Then consider how you arrived there, all round the convoluted corners and kinks of the dipper, including a period when you appeared to be traveling in precisely the opposite direction! When I see the Big Dipper, I see the whole course of our human history and our quest for God, and I see my own little journey in there too, meandering wildly at times, but ultimately, and certainly, leading me home to where I truly AM.

SUGGESTIONS FOR PRAYER AND REFLECTION 6

A Starlit Journey

After Jesus had been born at Bethlehem in Judaea during the reign of King Herod, some wise men came to Jerusalem from the east. "Where is the infant king of the Jews?" they asked. "We saw his star as it rose and have come to do him homage. . . ."

Then Herod summoned the wise men to see him privately. He asked them the exact date on which the star had appeared, and sent them on to Bethlehem. "Go and find out all about the child," he said, "and when you have found him, let me know, so that I too may go and do him homage."

Having listened to what the king had to say, they set out. And there in front of them was the star they had seen rising; it went forward and halted over the place where the child was.

The sight of the star filled them with delight, and going into the house they saw the child with his mother Mary, and falling to their knees they did him homage. Then, opening their treasures, they offered him gifts of gold and frankincense and myrrh. But they were warned in a dream not to go back to Herod, and returned to their own country by a different way.   (Matthew 2:1–2, 7–12)

Try to imagine yourself alongside these stargazers. Let the picture unfold to you. Recall the first sighting of that special star—your own North Star. Relive the excitement of that discovery and the certainty that this journey must be made, that it will lead you to the pearl of great price.

In prayer, make your own journey now, following that special star. Notice the landscape of your journey, your companions, the sights and sounds and smells of the countryside and the townships through which your journey leads you. Can you still see the star? How do you feel? What are you hoping for?

On your journey there are times of pure joy. Remember them and thank God for them. There are also times when you feel threatened, as the Magi did. Can you name any of those times now and lay your feelings before God, exactly as they are, undisguised?

As your journey moves on, you gradually learn to discern between what can be trusted and what cannot. What has helped you make this discernment? When was your discernment right? When did it let you down? Can you see any reasons for this?

Now imagine your arrival. Your North Star has come to rest above the place where your deepest desire lies. How do you react? Live the scene out now in your prayer and let your destination speak to you.

TRY DRAWING YOUR OWN life map, showing the terrain of your innermost self. What paths tend to lead you into desolation? What is the landscape of your consolation like? What trees grow in your forest of gifts? Where are your prayer pools? Are they full and flowing, or do they feel dry? What rivers feed them, bringing you encouragement and grace? There is no limit to what might appear on your life map. Populate it as you wish; it is for your eyes only.

NOW TAKE A WALK beneath the night sky. Let your prayer reveal the personal constellations by which you can plot your course. Draw your own pictures, either in your mind or on paper, of the constellations and what they mean to you. Include your own unique star-pointers—those things in your life that warn you that you are moving off course, and those that affirm your direction as true north.

DRAW YOUR OWN Big Dipper. At what times in your life did your journey seem, with hindsight, to be leading you in the wrong direction? How do you feel about your direction now? Is there any way in which you would wish to correct your course? The shape of your journey might not look like the Big Dipper. Try drawing the shape you feel your life is taking, maybe putting dates against crucial phases that you remember on your inner journey and naming significant events or people.

7

THE DEEPEST DESIRE

D ESIRE IS NOT easy to draw . . . not easy to describe . . . not easy to think about . . . not easy to live with.

Yet we are told that desire is the source of our vital energy and that our inner journey is focused—consciously or unconsciously—on our deepest desire. It also seems to be the case that the coin of our deepest desire has a reverse face, where our deepest fear is imprinted.

What does desire mean for us? Is it really so crucially important? How do we come to terms, creatively, with this seething mass of conflicting needs and hopes, dreams, dreads, and longings that we find in our hearts?

In this chapter we will not be seeking definitions or explanations. Instead, I will share with you a few pictures that have helped me to get in touch with my deepest desires, and that I hope may strike a chord with you, too.

The Thrust of Our Desiring

Desire is a strong word, full of energy. When we encounter our desires, we know that we are dealing with something forceful. *Thrust* seems to be the right word. Desires force themselves into our consciousness, whether we invite and encourage them or try to bar our mental doors against them. If we suppress them, they simply go underground, like bramble roots, and surface somewhere else when we least expect them. We don't need to be psychologists to recognize the power of this phenomenon in our lives.

It all reminds me of the thrust of growth we find in nature. For a tree, the thrusting goes in two directions. The life force inside the tree thrusts roots deep down into the ground, seeking water and nutrients. At the same time, the above-ground growth is thrusting branches out into the air, seeking the light and warmth of the sun and the life-giving components of the air. In the downward thrust of its roots, the tree obtains its nourishment and its firm hold in the earth. In the upward thrust of its branches, it reaches for light and warmth, but it also expresses, in a visible form, the truth and beauty of its own unique being.

It seems to me that our desires are a lot like that. When I look at the nature of my own desires, I see these two directions of thrust:

- desires that delve deep down, seeking hold and nourishment and security, I call these my *root desires,* and
- desires that urge me to express myself, to spread out my arms and my heart to the world around me and to my friends and loved ones; to reach out to those things that embody light and warmth for me—those things that delight me and warm my heart. I call these my *branch desires*.

A few examples might help to clarify this. Among my *root desires* I find such things as:

- a desire for safety and comfort; a desire for a stable home and a peaceful world in which I can be rooted,
- a desire for physical, mental, and spiritual nourishment,
- a desire to belong to a network of loving and accepting friends, who hold me in equilibrium even when outer circumstances get difficult,
- a thirst always to go deeper, for example, in friendship, in study, in prayer.

And among my *branch desires* I find:

- a desire to do work that is creative, that expresses the "real me" in the outside world,
- a desire to express, to trusted friends, the deepest feelings and hopes and dreams of my heart,
- a desire to show my compassion when I meet someone in distress, to open my heart toward them,
- a desire to go somehow "outside" and "beyond" myself when I am deeply moved, for example, by a piece of music or a starlit night.

You might like to reflect on your own root-and-branch desires. Try to be as specific as you can. This will ground your desires and help you get in touch with the tangible nature of them. The exercise is only valuable if it reveals actual desires, not abstract concepts.

We could say that one thing our desires do for us is prove that the universe (or even our own personal world) is not centered on ourselves. There is always something beyond, toward which our living energy is striving, delving down for security, stability, peace, nourishment, encouragement, companionship, and intimacy, and reaching out for creative self-expression, for the joy of responding to other forms of creativity, for fruitfulness and expansiveness. Tree roots go deep because there is always something deeper to strive for. Its branches reach up because the sky, the sun, and the air are always beyond and out of reach.

Yet it is precisely in the striving that the growth and the fruitfulness happen. It is in our seeking that we are found.

Identifying Our Deepest Desire

By now you are probably well aware of the kinds of desires that are milling around in your own heart. You have perhaps been able to name them specifically and recognize something of their nature as well as your own ways of responding to them. However, this still seems a long way from being able to recognize where these desires have their deepest roots. We all know the experience of desire, and the certainty that if and when we attain what we desire, we will still remain, at a deep level, unsatisfied.

St. Augustine expressed this feeling: "You made us for yourself, and our hearts find no peace until they rest in you."

It's as if every desire that we can experience and name points beyond itself. And where is that "beyond"? Well, we will surely not, in our human form, be able to reach that ultimate "beyond," but our deepest desire will bring us, perhaps, as close to it as the human spirit might venture. Most important, we will discover that we find our deepest desire not in our arriving but in our journeying; not in the finding but in the searching. "Seek and you will find" (or rather, you will be found, by the One who is seeking you) in the very heart of the searching.

And how, in practice, might we come to recognize those deep desires that touch the heart of our being? I would like to share two practical methods with you, which I call *Outside In* and *Inside Out*. The Outside-In method begins with the desires we know we have, or have had, in our conscious living. The Inside-Out method begins rather in the depths of ourselves with desires that we have only dimly sensed but never named, and to which we have access via myth and fairy tale.

Outside In

In the Outside-In method, we recall some of the desires that have dominated our hearts at different times of our lives. I have called it Outside-In because it starts with the desires we know we have or have had at different times, and leads us deeper into the underlying longings that these desires are expressing.

I remember, for example, when I was thirteen, desperately longing for a dog and a bike. These desires were more than just "Christmas wish list" desires; they had some driving passion in them. What was it? When my parents did indeed buy a puppy and give me a secondhand bike for my fourteenth birthday, at first I was delighted, but ultimately, the deep desire I had felt still remained unfulfilled and was displaced by

> What is it that we are really long-
> ing for but never quite find? Do we
> begin to find it in those moments
> when we experience the deep
> peace and solidity of consolation?
> Perhaps it is when we notice God
> gradually unfurling his reality in
> our own Who center.

the next heart dream. So if the puppy and the bike were not the real roots of those desires, what was?

Now, in prayer and with hindsight, I can see that in the puppy I was seeking companionship for a lonely childhood, and in the bike the real desire was for a new degree of freedom and independence. Both of these desires were partially fulfilled. Yet the days came when there were real human companionship and full adult independence and still I remained unfulfilled. Still I hadn't fully grasped the root of my deepest desire.

Take a moment to reflect on any desires that you can identify like this, perhaps from childhood or in careers or relationships. Our desires, like our moods, have deep, hidden roots, and if we follow these roots to their first origins (given that our directedness is toward God), will we not discover that all our deeply felt desires, at their true source, will be connected with our desire for God himself and our desire to become the person he is dreaming into being in our Who center?

Desires like "I want to stop smoking" or "I want to quit my job," for example, might be traced back to a deeper desire to be free. Desires such as "I want a baby" or "I want to refurbish the house" might be rooted in a deeper desire to be needed. And both of these deeper desires — to be free and to be needed — stem from the same root desire: "I want to be me."

Inside-Out

The Inside-Out method offers us a rather different way of getting in touch with our own deepest desires. Indeed, these desires and longings seem to run through all human experience, and in them we find our own dreams located. This is the method of fairy tale. Absurd as it may appear at first sight, we can begin to get in touch with our own heart dreams simply by picking up one of those discarded fairy-tale books that we once read to our children or grandchildren, or that we still cherish from our own childhood.

I have called this the Inside-Out method because fairy tales take us right to the heart of our desiring by way of pictures, symbols, and metaphors, and help us to connect these deep and universal desires (and fears) to the feelings we are experiencing in our own particular circumstances.

To try this method, sit back and relax and let your memory roam over the fairy tales that come to mind from your childhood. Does a particular favorite story come to mind? You may like to bring it into prayer by consciously asking God to show you what its meanings are telling you about your own desires and about his desire for you.

We could look together at a few examples. The first type is the "becoming who I really am" story, and we can see this meaning in the stories of "The Ugly Duckling" or "Cinderella." Is there an ugly duckling in you? Have you glimpsed the swan? Do you feel drawn to ask God to "grow" you from the duckling you feel like now to the swan you dream of becoming in him?

A second type of story is the "free me from the evil spell" story. We can see this in such tales as "Sleeping Beauty." These stories give us inner space in which to experience the coming of the Prince who recognizes our deepest needs and feels such compassion and love for us that he will risk his life to set us free from the spell that leaves us unable to help ourselves. You might like to take such a story into your prayer and let God speak his personal word to you there. He may be waiting for an opportunity to convince you of how much he loves you, or to reveal to you the seriousness of the spell that holds you, or even to engage your cooperation in taking risks to free others from their spells.

Then there is the "just one wish" story. Think of King Midas, who wished that everything he touched would turn to gold. Ponder before God what you would wish for if you could ask God to grant you just one of your desires. What is this one wish showing you about the things that you are most deeply hoping and longing for in your life? Let yourself be Cinderella, and receive your fairy godmother into your imagination. What ball do you want to go to? And why do you want to go so much? For a good night out? To get back at the ugly sisters in your life?

Or because you feel drawn toward the possibility of real and lasting transformation?

And finally, perhaps the most powerful story of all, that we find, for example, in the Frog Prince, is the "love changes everything" story. Do you feel like a frog most of the time? Deep down are you inclined to think that no one would really like you if they really knew you? Now let the princess rest her all-knowing gaze upon you. Let her give you the transforming kiss, however difficult, however impossible it feels. Let yourself be loved by the only one who really knows you, because he made you for his own.

All this sounds like news that is far too good to be true! And, yes, the fears and shadows that lurk around our hearts are not dismissed by the wave of a magic wand. There is, inevitably, a Humpty Dumpty sitting precariously on the walls of our lives, likely to fall apart at any moment! And all our king's horses and all our king's men won't get us together again. At best we might manage a rather shell-shocked omelette. But what God promises is a chick pecking its way out of our broken shells to something new!

In many ways, these familiar stories are Gospel stories, with considerable power to reveal to us who we really are and who we are longing to become. They occur in all cultures and languages, with remarkably similar detail, precisely because they are about the desires that lie at the roots of all human hoping and striving.

Confronting the But Bird

These practical exercises may have helped you to recognize the patterns of your own desires—what you wish you were, what you wish you possessed, what you dream of doing or becoming—and the deeper underlying roots of these desires.

We go on now to consider what it is that seems to stop these desires from reaching fulfillment. Remember, we are talking here of the matters that stir our hearts at the deepest levels, not daydreams like "I wish I could go to the moon, but I can't afford the fare." An example may help: I have a colleague who is a very gifted amateur artist but whose drawings were largely confined to the margins of his notepad in the form of doodles during boring meetings. A number of people commented on his talent, but he always continued to put himself down. However, the invitations to him to draw something began to multiply, from the parish magazine to a set of illustrations for a book. Just before the book went to press, he confided that it had been a lifelong dream of his to illustrate a book. Yet he had never told anyone of this dream, not even, I suspect, himself. And he had never done anything actively to bring about its realization. Why not?

What is it that stops us from acknowledging our dreams and seeking to fulfill them? Whatever the reasons in my colleague's case, a couple of general suggestions might be considered:

- We do not believe in ourselves, even though we say we believe in our Creator. We seem to harbor the notion that although God declared his work to be "good," we alone are "rejects." Sometimes, just announcing ourselves to be rubbish isn't good enough; we have to be the worst rubbish of all. But God doesn't, as someone once said, make junk.
- We do believe in ourselves, deep down, but we are afraid that other people might not. We are afraid of exposing ourselves to public opinion. We are afraid to risk our talent on the open market. And the fear is stronger than our desire to exercise our gifts fruitfully.

Perhaps we can get to the root of our fears in the same way that we probed our desires. As a practical exercise, try looking back over the last twenty-four hours again. Were there any moments when you felt a sudden stab of anxiety about something? Was there something around during that period that seemed to be clouding you over with a sense of foreboding or worry? Perhaps something jumped inside you when the phone rang or there was a knock at the door. Perhaps you read something, heard a conversation, saw something on television that summoned up a wall of resistance in you. Maybe you were asked to do something or go somewhere, and you realized that the very thought of doing so brought you up against an inner brick wall. Or possibly, you felt an impulse to do something and then stopped yourself, thinking,

> My fears outweigh my desire,
> My fears hold me down,
> My fears refuse to let me grow, to
>   let me fly, to let me be ME!
> The bird in my heart wants to fly,
>   free and high, but my fears clip
>   its wings and keep it earthbound.
> Where shall I align myself?
> With the good or the bad spirits?
> With the desires or the fears?
> With the positive or the negative
>   energies?
> In everything I do, I have a choice.

"I couldn't. . . ." Ask God to show you what, or who, lay at the root of those feelings.

As an example, let's consider the mother of a small child who goes out to a concert. She finds she isn't really enjoying the concert because she is worried about whether the child is all right and whether the concert will finish in time for her to be home at the time she promised the babysitter. She is only aware of some general unease within herself that is distracting her from the music. What might be at the root of it? Perhaps there are fears about her own judgment—is the babysitter reliable? Or about the relationship with her child—what if he wakes and finds me gone? Or maybe there are feelings of guilt about going out at all, or even about enjoying herself. Such fears could even be pointing to a damaging image of God as a figure of threat and punishment. Whatever they are, they are taking her over and undermining her enjoyment of the concert.

Our fears, then, are perhaps the worst enemies of our desires. If we could imagine them as sentient beings, we might come to the conclusion that they are waging a deliberate, lifelong campaign against the fulfillment of the God dream in us, as it is expressed in our own deepest desires.

On the side of the positive energies (my desires), the But Bird might have strong wing feathers, but on the side of the negative energies (my fears), the corresponding parts of the wing have been clipped. For example:

"I want to say how I really feel" might have been clipped by "but I might destroy our friendship."

"I want to give you a present" might have been clipped by "but you might misunderstand my motives."

"I want to do something different" might have been clipped by "but I might lose my security."

"I want to say, 'I love you'" might be forever suppressed by "but you might reject me."

Ignatius calls such negative inner movements the *false spirits* inside us, and he calls the positive movements the *good spirits*. The discernment process is the ongoing task of learning to recognize when we are being driven by the false, negative, destructive spirits and when we are being drawn by the good, positive, creative spirits in our hearts. Once discernment is being practiced prayerfully in the ways we have explored, it becomes possible to start consciously feeding the wholesome plants and to stop watering the weeds. It also becomes possible to make decisions with a greater degree of freedom.

SUGGESTIONS FOR PRAYER AND REFLECTION   7

God, you are my God, I am seeking you,
my soul is thirsting for you,
my flesh is longing for you,
a land parched, weary and waterless.   (Psalm 63:1)

LET THESE WORDS soak into your heart, as you sit, silent and relaxed, in God's presence. Imagine yourself as a sponge, soaking up God's love for you. Feel him filling your heart. Feel the living water trickling through the highways and byways of your life—through your experience of living today.

Notice how you are feeling. Notice especially those parts of your being that feel "worn out and waterless." How does the living water affect them? In your prayer, lay them down, without fear or disguise, before God, and express to him, in a way that feels right for you, your own response to him.

TRY DRAWING YOUR OWN life tree. Name those feelings and longings in yourself that you would see as root desires and those that are branch desires.

REMEMBER, IF YOU CAN, one or two things in your life that you have really longed for. Can you identify now what deeper needs and longings lay beneath these desires?

DO YOU HAVE a favorite fairy tale? If you do, remember it in your prayer, and relive it in your imagination. Is it opening up a personal story in your heart? If so, let it become a Gospel story for you.

WHAT SECRET DREAMS or ambitions do you cherish? What is it that prevents you from fulfilling them? Try setting your dreams alongside the blocks that "clip their wings." Do you want to stay with the blocks? If not, how might you encourage the positive movement in your life more strongly? Bring your feelings and your fears into prayer.

WRITE A SHORT wish list of things you hope for right now. Try tracing these things back, to see which branch of your desires is supporting them and where they really have their origins.

8 ⊚

WHY DON'T YOU ANSWER
MY PRAYERS?

T HERE WAS A time when I thought of my prayers as some kind of
lottery. I might get lucky on a few of my scratchboard prayers and
clock up a few ticks, as if I were checking God off against a shopping
list. Big wins were a lot less likely—really only dreams. Some people
even keep diaries of the answers they feel they have, or have not, received
to their specific prayers.

Today, though, I really question this way of thinking of prayer and
the ways in which God responds to it. To explain what I mean, we need
to go back to our thoughts on the "deepest desire." An image may help
here. We could imagine our deepest desire as a powerful underground
stream. Indeed, there are many images of exactly such a stream in
Scripture (for example, Ezekiel's stream, or Jesus' promise of living
water). This stream is so deep in our hearts that for the most part we are
not even aware of it ourselves. Remember how difficult it was to get in
touch with the deepest longings of our hearts when we tried to identify
our deepest desire. But this stream does show itself sometimes in the
conscious levels of our lives. Like a mountain stream, it bubbles up in
small springs and little fountains and trickles along the way. It seeps out
of rock faces, and it feeds our mountain flowers.

These visible signs of the underground flow of our hearts could be seen as the desires we know we have. These trickles may show themselves as areas of our experience where we are consciously striving for some specific happiness or success or fulfillment; for example, the strong desire to get a good job (or to get a job at all), to find a partner, to travel the world, to have a child, and so on. Or they may be more obvious by their absence. We may notice dry patches in our lives, and empty spaces, and ask God, in prayer, to fill them and take away the empty aching or the source of specific pain in ourselves or in others.

But all the while the deep current flows on, holding our deepest desire, often unspoken and unrecognized. Without trying too hard to identify what, exactly, it really holds in its depths, let us, rather, for a while in prayer simply be present to its existence, its power, and above all, its benevolence.

And I discover, when I let my prayer become this deep flow that I can't even name or ever fully know, the amazing truth that God is continuously responding to it, much as the parent of a much loved, much wanted child is continuously aware of the child's fundamental needs. The parent is continuously attending to those needs even though the child is unaware of them, and even when the child expresses "wants" that will not further his or her real interests and may even be damaging.

A strange reversal follows from this discovery. If I believe that God is continuously responding to my deepest desire, then it follows that by observing God's action in my life and his movement in my heart, I will be able to see more and more clearly what my deepest desires really are. Paradoxical though it may appear, I will become able to hear my prayers by listening to the answers, and not the other way around.

In a sense, this is another manifestation of the Copernican revolution: my prayer, I find, is not really mine at all but rather expresses the movements of my deepest underground streams and currents that spring from God and are known and understood fully only by him. God's answers are not brought about by my prayer at all, any more than the sun's movements are determined by the earth's. Rather, my prayer is the response to God's action in my life and his presence in my heart, just as the earth's existence is a *response* to the sun's.

In the previous chapter we looked at ways of getting in touch with what this deep current of desire is really about in our personal experience. We now consider two areas of choice that we face with regard to these deep currents:

- the choice about how we respond to our desires, and
- the choice about which desires we will choose to follow.

What we discover about the way we are making these choices can reveal a great deal to us about how God is answering our prayers through what he is doing in our lives, even though it doesn't always look like it.

The way we respond to our desires can determine whether our desiring is, ultimately, diminishing or expanding us. The decision about which desires we will pursue reveals the conflicts inherent in our desiring, and the way that conflict gets resolved according to our own choices.

A Word about Feelings

Our feelings are conscious signs of our desires. They are the first pointers to what our hearts are most deeply desiring or fearing, but they are also, according to psychologists, the source of our energy. If you doubt this, remember how things were with you when you first fell in love, and how the energy released in you made you think you could take on the whole world.

We don't have a choice about the feelings we experience—they simply are there. But we *do* have a choice about how we focus the energy they generate, and about whether we choose to nourish them or discourage them. We could say that the feelings themselves are in the Where layer of our lives, our response to them lies within the scope of the How layer, and the ultimate effect of our choices makes a difference to the Who at our center, which is where transformation happens.

The process of sifting out the deepest desire (and letting the others lessen in importance) could be seen as a process of energy focusing.

Just as a winter tree directs all its energies to the nurturing of its roots
and its new, unseen growth, and the summer tree focuses its energy on
the production of leaf, flower, and fruit in order to reproduce itself, so
our energy lines will vary through the stages of our lives, reflecting the
movements of our deeply felt desires. There is a natural cycle in energy
directing that is mirrored in the cycles of our spiritual growth.

The most obvious detonation of positive energy that we can ever
know is the Easter Resurrection energy that released, and continues to
release, life out of death. The root of that explosion was surely love. Are
our desires perhaps ultimately rooted in love and in the desire for union
with the God who is love? And do our deepest fears perhaps have to do
with the awareness of the possibility of alienation from that source of
love, and the eternal emptiness of an abyss of lovelessness?

You might like to return now to any powerful feelings you have experienced recently, and ask God to show you the energy they are generating, whether it is positive or negative, how you are directing it, and
how you might be able to direct it more effectively.

Give or Take: Responding to Our Desires

Our striving and desiring are always toward something beyond ourselves, but we have a choice about how we respond to our desires. One
way of looking at this choice is to see our responses as either *taking* or
giving. Taking desires boil down to a kind of inner consumerism. There
is something that I desire, so I apply my energies to possessing the desired object. This might be something wholly legitimate, like a bar of
chocolate, a book, or a pair of shoes. Or it might be less tangible, like a
job or a qualification, that can't just be reached out for and taken. Or—
and here the desire to possess becomes illegitimate—it might be a
beloved person. Whatever it is, I have recognized a desire within myself
and I am inclined to take steps to draw that desired object into myself.

A familiar example of this mindset is the phrase that we often hear
and may well use ourselves: "We had weekend in Paris and *took* in the
Eiffel Tower, Montmartre, and a couple of museums." It might be worth
reflecting on what this kind of language says about the way we view the

world around us. It sounds harmless enough in itself, but is it about taking or giving, about consuming or responding?

Giving desires work the other way around. They do the drawing. Recall for a moment the feeling you experience when you listen to a piece of music that moves you deeply, or when you see a sunset or a star-filled sky, or when you gaze at a newborn child. Something tugs inside you and says: "This is something utterly wonderful, and quite beyond yourself. You can never possess it, and you don't want to, because to possess it would be to spoil it." Your response forces you to let the object of desire be itself, quite other, quite transcendent. There could never be enough space inside you to take in the object of your experience, even if you were to try. But the feeling remains one of desire.

There is a desire to experience this powerful feeling, this relationship, with what is drawing you toward itself. There is also a desire to respond in some way, and often that response will come in the form of a leap of joy experienced somewhere in the gut. You feel that you have been expanded by the experience, but the object of your desire has not thereby been diminished. You also feel that the object of your desire has drawn something out of the center of your own heart, yet you know that you have not been lessened, but, paradoxically, expanded inwardly by this drawing out.

This difference has to do with what Ignatius meant by "ordered" vs. "disordered" desires. Ordered desires expand us without diminishing the other. They draw us into a creative relationship with what lies beyond ourselves without tempting us to try to possess it. They represent a moving out of ourselves, a surrendering of something in our hearts to the power of the "other." They spur us on to new steps along the inner journey. They lead toward transformation.

Disordered desires behave in the opposite way. They tempt us to suck things into ourselves, and result in the diminishment of the desired object. When I desire an orange and take it into myself, the orange ceases to be an orange and becomes a part of me instead. This may be fine when all I desire is a piece of fruit, but if my desire is focused on another human person, this kind of response to my desire becomes destructive. It destroys my relationship with the person, and ultimately, it destroys me, too, as I pursue my desire obsessively and become more and more compulsive. More important, it can destroy the desired person by suffocating them with my own feelings, unless they have the wisdom to withdraw from me to a safe distance.

We could take a spider as a model of desiring that is ultimately destructive, while a bee demonstrates a different, creative way of desiring and of fulfilling that desire. Whatever comes into the spider's web (which we could compare to the force fields of our own personality) is consumed. It is taken into the spider, as into a black hole, and destroyed. The spider satisfies itself at the expense of what it desires.

The bee, on the other hand, feels attracted to what gives it joy. The bee seeks the nectar and receives the pollen, but it leaves the flower undiminished. The bee is filled, and the flower is pollinated. Both the bee and the flower are enriched by the encounter. Can you identify any of your own desires and your responses to them with either the spider model or the bee model?

Survival of the Fittest: Choosing Which Desires to Follow

A change of scene now: not the forest anymore, but the football field, and the start of the season, when every hopeful team is looking longingly toward the Super Bowl.

When I reflect on my desires, I can imagine myself at the start of the season. If I were asked to write a list of the things I want, the things I hope for, the things I dream of, there would probably be as many of them as there are hopeful starters in the National Football League. You might like to try this exercise and see whether you can identify any of your teams!

How, out of all this chaos, is the deepest desire ever to come through and rule my heart? I seem to be faced with a disorderly mob of wants and wishes, and their negative counterparts, my fears and resistances, and when I stop to look at them, I find that they are even in conflict with each other. A few examples:

- I want to take that new job, but I don't want to move.
- I want to lose weight, but I want to eat my favorite food.
- I want to speak up about that injustice at work, but I want to retain the good opinion of my colleagues.
- I want to belong to the Church, but I object to some of the ways it does things.

The list of potential conflicts is endless, and yet the way in which they get sifted, in a kind of evolutionary process, is as clear and straightforward as the way teams either get eliminated from the championships or go forward to the next round.

It happens in every choice we make!

As with computers, our choosing seems to work on a binary system. We may feel that a choice is full of compromise, but if we examine it critically, we will invariably find that we always choose the preferred course between two (or more) options.

A radical way of expressing this is to assert that no one ever does what they don't choose to do.

This sounds preposterous on the surface, and the choice may well be between the lesser of evils, but I have found this statement to be true in my everyday choices, and even in a situation where there appears to be no choice. Under threat of violence, for example, it still holds: "I desire to stay alive more than I desire to express my opposition." Some people have made the opposite choice in such circumstances, of course, and become martyrs for their convictions.

It's easy to see how this logic operates in the unimportant matters. If I want to lose weight badly enough, I will give up some of my favorite fattening foods. Then the weight-loss desire wins the match and goes on to the next round. There it may meet a stronger opponent; for example, "Do I want to keep on losing weight even if that means dropping all the business lunches?" And so on.

It's less easy to see it in the bigger issues. Consider this dilemma: I can't come to visit you because I can't drive. The two teams playing here are: my desire to visit you (a positive feeling) vs. my fear of driving (a negative feeling). The choice is mine. If I want to visit you badly enough, I will overcome my fear of driving. And if I do, my fear of driving will be weakened, and next time my positive choices for mobility will have a better chance of winning. The survivor will always be the stronger desire.

One thing is worth noticing in all of this: the choice is ours. It isn't anyone else's fault if I don't choose what I want. My own heart has the full freedom, and the responsibility, of the choice, even though I may think I am acting under coercion. This makes it sound disarmingly simple. In a way it is, but of course we all know that in practice it can be terribly hard, and sometimes impossible, in our fallen state, to make the choices we really want to make. But knowing our desires is at least a step along the way to choosing their fulfillment.

Try looking back now on some of the choices (big and small) that you have made recently, and see for yourself which desire has won in each case. Can you discern a pattern in your choice making?

For example, you may have chosen to phone a friend instead of reading another chapter of your novel or to spend your lunch hour listening to a colleague's problems instead of finishing a job that was running late. Such choices indicate your tendency to value friendship more than personal achievement.

On the other hand, you may have chosen to keep a low profile in a contentious discussion instead of expressing your opposition to an injustice, or to put off saying something difficult instead of replying to a challenging letter immediately. These choices could indicate that you fear confrontation more than you value directness and honesty.

When I start to touch on the deeper desires and fears that underpin my surface wishes and aversions, I start to narrow the field. The rabble of village teams that started at the beginning of the season moves closer to the quarter-finals or even the semi-finals. The contenders are fewer, but the conflict seems to be more intense. There is big money involved now. The contest is for my heart, and there are no holds barred. I begin to understand why my deepest desire is such a vital question on my inner journey and to appreciate the scale of the conflict.

God's Will and Our Desire: The Key to Transformation

Now seems to be a good point to pause and draw together the conclusions of all that we have been reflecting on in this and the previous chapter. When we do so, we may discover an amazing surprise. "God's will," which for years we had imagined as some secret coded message locked up somewhere in the Fort Knox of the Church's treasury, may suddenly become blindingly obvious to us! Let me explain how we come to this discovery:

- Among all my multitude of desires there are patterns evolving. It is possible to identify which of my desires run deep, which are forming my choices and transforming me.

- In the struggle of my desires, I am choosing, minute by minute, the particular desire that is the stronger in me. Every time I choose in favor of my deeper desire, I reinforce it. It becomes dominant, until it meets an even stronger desire in me. In this way, my lived experience gradually reveals to me my own deepest desires.

- I am directed toward God (fundamentally). It follows that my deepest desire is centered on becoming the person God created me to be (whatever that means for me in practice). However, as we saw in earlier chapters, even though I am fundamentally directed toward God, there will be movements and choices in me that are going in the opposite direction. What I choose in times of desolation (when I am temporarily turned away from God) will not be in line with my deepest desire. This is why we are warned not to let desolation change our course, and not to go back on choices we made when we were in consolation.

- Because my real state is one of consolation and God-directedness, when I am really living true, my own deepest desire (to become the person God created me to be) is in complete harmony with God's will for me (that I might become the person he created me to be). God's will, therefore, becomes not something remote and unknowable (that I will be punished for not carrying out!) but something as close to me as the deepest desire of my own heart, and something that he is only waiting and longing to reveal to me in every moment of my life and in every breath of my prayer. God's will—his desire for me—and my own deepest desire (when I am really living true) are one and the same thing!

It follows that:

- Because God is continually carrying out his wil—his desire—for his creation (in spite of our obstructions!), I can be sure that he will always be doing, in my life, things to further that deep desire.
- If I notice and attend to what God (through the positive movements, the good spirits of my living) is actually doing in my life, this will show me what my deepest desire really is. It will also reveal God's will for me — and I don't need a map of the minefield after all!

This brings us back to the burning question with which this chapter began: "Why don't you answer my prayers?"

Now I can answer that question with a degree of painful honesty: "You *are* answering my prayer because you are continually nurturing the deepest desire of my heart (though I might not be doing so myself!), which is also your deepest desire for me and your will for me.

"If it doesn't feel like that, then let me reexamine, in prayer, those areas of my experience where I feel you are not answering my prayer, and see whether these areas are, truly, about my deepest desires or rather about the lesser desires that would sap my energy and distract me from my search for you and for my own deepest truth."

In the Eye of the Storm

All this discovery of the mortal combat going on in me between my mass of conflicting desires might, you would think, point toward a terrible final confrontation between my warring inner factions.

The good news is that quite the opposite appears to happen. In my own journeying, at least, I find that when I feel I am somehow touching on that which my heart most deeply desires (even though I may not be able to put a name to it), I experience a profound sense of peace. It may be fleeting and momentary, but it is truly there; it has the same quality as the sense of true north that we explored in earlier chapters. Conversely, I learn that when I experience such a sense of peace, I am close to touching on my deepest

> At the center of myself, where I am utterly vulnerable, there is my deepest desire, and my deepest desire is unarmed.

desire, and if I stop to reflect on what has brought me to this point, I may catch a glimpse of the nature of my deepest desire.

Why should this be? When all the desires (and fears) clamoring around my outer layers seem armed to the teeth and fighting for supremacy, causing turmoil in my heart, how can it be that when I penetrate the deepest levels of myself, I find a singleness of desire and longing that is deeply at peace?

This is not the peace of the victor over the vanquished! It is rather the peace that grows when all the apparently conflicting desires of my heart have been named, faced, accepted, and integrated into who I really am. It is an inclusive peace, embracing all of me, not just the holy bits.

Ironically, it was through a robbery that I began to sense this possibility of peace and why it is unarmed. One Christmas while we were away on vacation, our home was burgled. The intruders ransacked every cupboard, including those in a quiet room that we use for prayer and for days of retreat. Some weeks later, this experience returned to me in prayer, and I was surprised to find that in this room I felt no sense of invasion, even though I knew that hostile strangers had searched through its cupboards. Nothing of their spirit lingered in the room. Then my prayer itself seemed to reassure me that there could be no invasion, no threat in such a place, even if they had stripped the room, because what was truly present there—the spirit of the place—was indestructible, and therefore had no need of arms or defenses.

But that prayer wasn't really about the prayer room. It was about my own inner room, my own reality, my Who center, my true center. It was about that heart of me where I feel utterly vulnerable because there are no defenses there. And there are no defenses there because none are needed. I have no need to defend my Who center because, whatever is done to it, it is indestructible, just as God himself is indestructible.

Of course, most of the time we are aware only of the vulnerability we feel at our deepest center, and we are much less conscious of its indestructibility. Yet at moments when our deepest desire is touched and begins its transforming action within us, then we know peace—the peace that goes beyond all the struggle and supersedes it—the peace that passes understanding. In the eye of the storm is a center of perfect peace, where our deepest desire is embraced as God's own desire for us.

When we experience these moments of peace, we are experiencing a meeting point with God that will reveal to us where and how transformation is beginning to happen within us. It is the space where we discover answers to the prayers we have not yet found the words to form, where we are forgiven for sins we have not yet recognized, and freed from prisons that we thought were pots of honey. That is where God is answering our prayers continuously, because that is where he is, and where he engages our reality with his own.

SUGGESTIONS FOR PRAYER AND REFLECTION   8

As they left Jericho a large crowd followed him. Now there were two blind men sitting at the side of the road. When they heard that it was Jesus who was passing by, they shouted, "Lord! Have pity on us, Son of David." And the crowd scolded them and told them to keep quiet, but they only shouted more loudly, "Lord! Have pity on us, Son of David." Jesus stopped, called them over and said, "What do you want me to do for you?"

(Matthew 20:29–32)

NOW LET JESUS COME to you, at the roadside of your journey.

He stops. . . .

He calls to you. . . .

"What do you want me to do for you?" . . .

How do you respond?

Can you identify any areas of your experience that are fueled by giving desires? Any that are dominated by taking desires? Where, in your experience, do you feel like a spider, and where do you feel like a bee? Take them into your prayer, and allow God to show you the difference between these two kinds of desiring and the effects they are having on your heart.

DURING THE COURSE of the day, you will have faced countless choices. Remember just a few of them now. Which desires (or fears) were engaged in these choices, and which were the winners? Can you see any pattern evolving in your choosing one course of action over another through the living of your day, or of your life in general?

REMEMBER SOME of the things you have been asking for in prayer recently. In what ways do you feel that these things connect to the deeper desires you are discovering in your heart? Now look back on the most obvious ways in which you feel God has been acting in your life recently. How do these ways connect to your deepest desires?

Have you experienced any moments of peace in the eye of the storm recently? If so, thank God for them in your prayer, and remember them as anchor points for future struggles.

CENTER YOURSELF deeply in prayer. Allow yourself to be drawn ever more deeply into the heart of your own being, where God is indwelling. In that space, where you are most truly yourself, allow Christ to die on the cross. Allow him to descend into hell. Allow him to walk across the resurrection garden, his arms outstretched toward you. Invite him to show you, in his perfect way for you, that your deepest reality is as indestructible as his own reality.

As he began his journey as a pilgrim of God, Iñigo, the former warrior, symbolically laid down his arms at the shrine of the Black Madonna in Montserrat. If you feel drawn to do so, offer your armor and defenses to God in your prayer. As you do so, name each piece of armor that you feel you are using to protect your vulnerable heart—each disguise, each mask, each attitude that you use to shield yourself against the pain of being a living, feeling being. We all need these shields to cope with the demands of life and of each other, but here, in your prayer, you are making this surrender to God alone, asking him to show you that your true center, though utterly vulnerable, no longer has any need of them, because it is his own dwelling place.

9

Recognizing Our
Attachments

WE HAVE SPENT quite some time with our desires—those two-edged swords that can either free us or enslave us. Without desire, there would be nothing to move us forward, as our energy is the product of our desires. If we had no desire for food, we would starve. If we had no desire to discover what lies beyond our range of vision, we would never take any steps at all, either with our feet or with our minds. It could even be said that the existence of our desires is proof that there is a "beyond" toward which we strive and that creation does not end at the boundaries of our own hearts.

God created us with our desires. To deny our desires is to deny our whole human nature and the purpose of our being. So when does a desire become an addiction? What is it that changes natural longings and strivings into destructive compulsions? I'm not a psychologist, and I'm not going to attempt to answer these questions scientifically. I am only a pray-er who has observed the pull of compulsions in herself and is learning to notice her inner compass, especially when it starts to wobble! Gradually, in prayer and over time, I am beginning to recognize when my addictions are commandeering my energy and when, by contrast, I am closer to my true north.

The Swing of the Pendulum

I discovered the difference between true north and the wobbles one night during a retreat. In the corridor close to my room, there was a big, old-fashioned grandfather clock. In the deep silence of the retreat house, which deepened even further at night, all I could hear in the corridor was the steady ticking of this clock. As I listened to its ticking, I used to imagine the long weight of the pendulum moving from side to side. It was this clock that taught me something of my own inner movements. My inner pendulum, I thought to myself, would be in perfect balance when it was hanging straight down, with no movement to either side. But this, I soon realized, was far from my normal state. More usually my pendulum was swinging out to one side or the other—often quite wildly. I recognized these swings as resulting from the pull of my attachments. There were *positive attachments* and *negative attachments,* things I excessively desired to have or to be, and things I excessively desired to avoid. As long as the pendulum swings in moderation and balance, the clock stays true to its purpose and keeps good time. But if it were to swing excessively to either side, it would lose all balance and become unreliable.

Note the word *excessively.* One way in which we can tell that a natural desire is becoming a compulsion or an addiction is when it starts to take us over, so that we begin to make our choices, not in inner freedom, but in the desire to gain what we want or in the fear of losing something or someone to the point that our lives are negatively affected. For example, we have a natural desire to be safe, healthy, and unharmed, but if this desire becomes excessive, so that we don't dare to go out of the house, then it has become compulsive. We have become the slave of our own desire, and we start to live in dependency upon it.

Watering the Weeds, or Nourishing the Crop?

Another way to look at our desires is to notice how we are focusing the energy they generate and whether this energy is fueling our onward journey toward wholeness in the life of God, or whether it is directed away from this life-giving journey. Suppose, for example, that I have an aversion (a negative attachment) to flying. This becomes compulsive if I begin to arrange my life around it, such as choosing not to visit friends overseas or not taking a job involving travel. If this happens, I can find that I am spending more energy on avoiding flying than I am on the positive, life-giving aspects of my life. In gardener's terms, I am watering the weeds while neglecting the main crop! I am attending more to the things that are *life denying* (my fears and aversions) than to the movements in me that are *life giving*. And I have surrendered something of my inner freedom and given myself over to a kind of slavery, dictated by my fear of flying.

The slave maker could also be a positive attachment. Perhaps I am excessively concerned with what people think of me and whether or not they like me. People have a natural desire to be liked and accepted. It becomes dominant and destructive, however, if it leads me to be insincere in the way I deal with people, in order to win their good opinion. Eventually, the insincerity I feel within myself will pull my pendulum out of balance.

A person who can teach us much about the imbalance our attachments cause in our hearts is Pontius Pilate. Imagine yourself at Jesus' trial. Pilate is torn in all directions: he wants to remain popular with the Jewish people, but he doesn't want to fall afoul of the Roman authorities and ruin his career. He wants to stay on good terms with his wife, who has warned him about her dream, and almost certainly he doesn't want to be associated with the violence against Jesus. His Who center is fragmented, and his various fears and desires are making his pendulum swing wildly backward and forward. As a result, his energy is unfocused and frenzied, and he makes the choice that is eternally life-denying. By contrast, Jesus himself is to hang in perfect balance on the cross, like a compass needle eternally steadied on true north, utterly dependent on God—the only dependency that is life giving.

The day after my night with the grandfather clock, I came upon a large crucifix on the grounds of the retreat house. As I stood there gazing at it, just as I had stood listening to the clock, something fell into place inside me, and I knew that my deepest desire had been touched by that picture of perfect balance. This was the opposite of my own (and Pilate's) fragmentation. This was a pointer to truth.

See whether you can identify any of your own positive or negative attachments. Notice how far they are pulling you out of balance and restricting your inner freedom to make choices in your life without inordinate hope of gain or fear of loss. Then reflect on the weeds and the crop growing in your heart's field, and on how much attention you are giving to the one and to the other.

The Discomforts of Being "Hooked"

Another step for me in recognizing my own addictedness to certain things, people, or circumstances came in the form of a language lesson and a picture. See whether either or both of them ring any bells in the depths of your experience.

- The language lesson: the English word *dependent* comes from the Latin verb *pendere,* meaning "to hang." The German word for *dependent* is *abhängig,* meaning "hanging down from."
- The picture: Imagine yourself hanging from a hook in the ceiling. You are clinging to the hook for dear life, terrified lest it should fail to hold you and cause you to fall into the fearful depths below.

Let's take a closer look at what it means to be hooked like this:

- See how all your energy and attention are focused on the overriding need to hold on to the hook.
- See how the need to grip the hook is distorting you, twisting your hand, and making you stiff and lopsided.
- Feel, in your imagination, the effects of hanging like this: the exhaustion, the strain, the stiff arm, the painful hand, the tension in your neck muscles, and so on. Your body is trying to tell you that it isn't designed to hang on one arm like this!

Can you name the hook(s) in your life? You might be aware of something—a person, relationship, ambition, or circumstance—in your life that you feel you couldn't possibly get by without. Then ask yourself (gently and compassionately) these questions:

> Natural interdependencies on one another and on our earth make us human. A "hook" dependency pulls us out of balance and prevents us from making choices in inner freedom.

- Does my happiness depend on _____ (the presence of another person, a particular event or circumstance or achievement), and is this need starting to dominate my consciousness and sap all my energy? Am I starting to arrange my life around it?
- If so, do I want it to be like this?

Consider again how it feels to be hooked. Just as our bodies are clearly not designed to hang by one arm, and our muscles would tell us that soon enough, so, too, our feelings will tell us if we are suffering from some emotional or spiritual addiction. We need only think of the turmoil and anxiety we feel when we are inordinately attached to someone or something—fear of the possibility of loss, a determination to cling—all these feelings are warning signals issued by our spiritual muscles to tell us that our Who center, our real self, is not designed for such dependency.

Yet it seems impossible to let go of the hook. It seems as though that will happen only when something or someone cuts us down or severs our wrist, or when the hook comes out of its anchor and literally lets us down in betrayal or disappointment. All of these possibilities are unthinkably painful, and our hearts close up against them. Characteristic of someone in the grip of an addiction, we prefer to deny the problem rather than face the pain of the cure. We might recall Jesus' warning: If your right hand causes you to sin (or to get hooked on a dependency that threatens your inner freedom), much better to cut it off than to freeze your whole being into an addicted state.

Now let your imagination go further to envision the worst scenario. The hook loosens and gives way, or some unexpected turn of events slashes your wrist and severs your hold on the hook. Perhaps you can remember times in your life when this happened to you, when something or someone you centered your need love on has been taken from you, possibly in the trauma of downsizing or in the breakup of a relationship. Feel yourself falling. Feel the ghastly drop from the ceiling to the floor. Feel the pain of your landing, the bruising and the broken feelings. But notice something else as well. Notice the solid floor underneath you, which, though hard and cold, is not a bottomless abyss after all. Try, in your imagination, to stand up on this solid ground. Notice your legs and feet, now free and able to walk again. See how it feels to put one foot in front of the other and walk forward. Once again you are free, free to walk on, an impossible dream as long as you were suspended from your hook in the ceiling. Let yourself feel the returning use of your legs. It is a hard-won and painful freedom, but it is freedom, and it signals growth.

Learning to Walk

I was reminded of this pain of becoming free one day when I was standing in line to take care of some business. As I waited, I watched the man in front of me, who was holding his toddler in his arms as he carried out his transaction. When he had to sign his name, he put the little boy down. Until that moment, the child had been lying peacefully in his father's arms, his head resting quietly on the broad, accepting shoulder. But when he was put down and required to stand on his own for a few moments, he let out a wail of protest and held up his arms to be picked up again.

As I watched this little scene, I could see events from my own life reenacted, in times when my steady certainties and assumed securities had been blown apart by unwelcome surprises, and I had found myself standing alone on a hard floor. What had happened to the comforting, sustaining arms that used to hold me? I have howled in protest and instinctively held up my arms to be taken back to safety.

I asked myself some questions that afternoon as I stood in line. I asked myself whether I really wanted to be a toddler all my life. And then I asked myself which way of being was the more secure—to be held safe but dependent, or to stand alone and take my chances in a world that might turn out to contain no certainties except my trust in the presence of God?

The man in front of me finished his transaction, picked up his little boy again, and a contented silence was restored. He carried his son out of the building, but I knew that I would have to walk. In my heart of hearts, I wanted to walk, even though the loss of my familiar comforts and securities was painful.

What Price Your Love? A Dialogue with Darkness

As a test of whether you have any addictions, try pondering this little story from the book of Job. I have adapted the original text from Job 1:6—22. Insert your own name at the appropriate points, and imagine that the dialogue is about you.

One day, Satan was having a chat with God.

"Where have you been?" God asked him.

"Round the earth," he replied, a touch defensively. "Roaming about!"

"Did you come across my friend _____ in your travels?" God inquired. "She's such a friend. She talks to me every day, and she's really trying to be the person I created her to be. You must have noticed her. I'm quite proud of her!"

"Oh, yes, I noticed her all right," Satan replied. "But you know, God, she's not your friend for nothing, is she?"

"What's that supposed to mean?" God asked, bristling warily.

Satan shrugged nonchalantly. "Only what I said," he remarked provocatively. "She's well looked after in her friendship with you. Look how you keep her safe and stable and in good health. Look at the good supportive friends she has (name some of your friends). Look at the gifts you have given her (name some of your gifts). Look at how you have given her the gift of prayer, and how you smile your blessing upon all she thinks she is doing for you and your Kingdom. I call that a real fat-cat salary for her friendship with you!"

God mused to himself for a while. Well, yes, he was fond of _____, and why wouldn't he bless her and encourage her, but Satan did have a point. . . .

Satan, always with an eye to the main chance, noticed this moment of hesitation and moved in with the heavy artillery.

"Just what do you think would happen to her discipleship if all of that went—disappeared, just like that, overnight? Any bets she would soon see the dark side of the moon and start to wonder whether her inner journey wasn't just an illusion? Worse, I reckon she would turn on you, and all her love would turn to spite!"

God was silenced. The thought shocked him. But he believed in _____ . Maybe he believed in her more than she in him. At any rate, he was ready to risk his faith in her, right to the limits.

"All right," he agreed. "You can do anything you like to her outer layers. You can break her certainties apart and take away everything she values. But you may not touch her Who center. That is sacred space. I give everything else of hers into your power."

Satan was delighted. He shot off like a bat out of hell before God could change his mind.

And poor _____ was in for a hard time. One after another, all the things she valued were stripped away from her. It began with the things she had thought she could well do without, such as _____ . It really hurt, after all, letting them go, but it didn't destroy her. Then the screws tightened, and things she had always thought were permanent started to shake (_____). It was then, when she thought she was in total desolation, that Satan struck the worst blows of all. She found herself bereft, overnight, of those things closest to her heart, things that seemed to be part of who she really, deeply was. Night fell, inside and out. There seemed no reason to go on living. There was no reason to stay with a so-called life-giving God whose consolations could run dry like that for no apparent reason.

She looked back to past times when desolation had hit her. She remembered times when she had given up on God before and plowed her own furrow instead. And then again she remembered times when she had stayed with the dream. It struck her that she had, after all, written her own script for living, and she was still free to write the script for the journey onward—or for the journey backward. Where did that freedom come from? she wondered. And why hadn't God shattered that as well, since he seemed to have it in for her?

So how does the story end? Does she stay with the darkness, or does she discover the free space still intact and unharmed in her Who center, where the next choice can still be freely made? Does Satan win the day, or is God's faith in his friend vindicated?

The Good News is that our journey with God is a journey into freedom. He invites us, over and over, to cut free from our inordinate attachments, and he does it with carrots, not with sticks, as we shall discover in the next chapter.

SUGGESTIONS FOR PRAYER AND REFLECTION 9

[Jesus] was setting out on a journey when a man ran up, knelt before him and put this question to him, "Good master, what must I do to inherit eternal life?" Jesus said to him, "Why do you call me good? No one is good but God alone. You know the commandments: You must not kill; You must not commit adultery; You must not steal; You must not bring false witness; You must not defraud; Honor your father and mother." And he said to him, "Master, I have kept all these from my earliest days." Jesus looked steadily at him and loved him, and he said, "There is one thing you lack. Go and sell everything you own and give the money to the poor, and you will have treasure in heaven; then come, follow me." But his face fell at these words and he went away sad, for he was a man of great wealth. (Mark 10:17–27)

TRY TO IMAGINE yourself as being present at this scene. Bring to your prayer your own longing for that "extra something" that would change your believing from a flicker to a flame.

Notice, prayerfully, how your heart's pendulum has been behaving today. Have there been any wild swings to either side? Any moments of perfect balance in true north? Does the pattern you notice indicate any larger pattern discernible in your life?

Ask the Lord to show you the blocks that are getting in the way of your relationship with him, and the hooks that are impeding your freedom to move forward with him. Ask him to show you your own personal "riches" —the baggage that is overloading you and preventing your passage "through the eye of the needle."

Let him speak to your heart, and listen to the suggestions that arise in your prayer. As he speaks to you, notice especially the expression in his eyes ("Jesus looked steadily at him, and *loved* him"), and hear his words: "Everything is possible *for God.*"

Can you recall any time when you felt absolutely certain about a particular course of action and went ahead with it in that inner certainty that it was right and true, knowing that, for once at least, you were following your truest instincts? Replay that incident now in prayer, and ask God to imprint in your heart the knowledge of how it really feels when your compass is reading true north, your pendulum is in balance, and you are living—and acting—true.

RECALL A DECISION you have made recently. Can you identify your reasons for deciding as you did? Did you decide in the hope of gaining something, in the fear of losing something, or out of a state of inner freedom?

IN YOUR IMAGINATION, take a walk around the field of your life. Notice the blessings, the gifts, and the fruitfulness, and give thanks to God for that "crop." Now notice any weeds that you know are there. Stand still, and give them over to God, as you would leave a sick child with a doctor. Now turn back to the crop again, and thank God for it, asking him to help you nourish it and share it.

CAN YOU IDENTIFY any hooks that are operating in your life? If so, name them to God in your prayer, and perhaps, if you feel able to do so, to a trusted human friend. Simply to recognize and own them is a significant step forward toward being free of them. If you can do this, you have passed beyond the stage of denial and have opened yourself up to healing.

HAVE THE CIRCUMSTANCES of your life ever cut you down from a hook, or some state of complacency or security, and left you bruised and frightened on a cold, hard floor? Now, with hindsight, can you remember how you first began to recover from that shock and take your first tentative steps forward on your own two feet? Bring this memory into prayer, asking God to help you recognize the possibility of journeying on to life-in-all-its-fullness and to trust this possibility into an unknown future. (If you do this exercise, don't do violence to yourself! If the memory is still too painful, leave it in God's care until you feel more comfortable reflecting on it.)

 10

PATHWAYS TO DETACHMENT

Is your "God" a policeman or a midwife? When you think of God, do you see a law-enforcement officer, determined to keep you on the straight and narrow, or do you see someone who knows you—and loves you, more than you know and love yourself—and is attending your birth into life-in-all-its-fullness?

I hope that, having come this far in exploring your journey with God, you will have discovered something of God's midwifery skills and his urgent, insistent call to freedom in your life—not the freedom that is the anarchy of lawlessness, but the freedom of the baby who leaves the restricting spaces of the womb to enter the immensity of life.

Of course, all our images of God are inadequate, and some can be dangerously wrong. But I find the midwife picture one of the more helpful ones. Perhaps we can let it lead us on into our reflections on what detachment might mean and how we can get closer to it.

For all of us, our first experience of the pain and the promise of detachment was the hour we left our mother's womb and, screaming with shock, entered human life on earth. In the seemingly brutal act of cutting the umbilical cord, which separated us from the prenatal food supply, we were in fact set free to live our own lives.

So it began, and so it continues in the ongoing call to let go of what is not (or is no longer) leading us closer to God, and to choose instead

those ways that for us personally lead closer to him and to the fulfillment of his dream of us.

The Meaning of Detachment

Ignatius urges us to seek the freedom of detachment or indifference.
Neither of these words carries weight in today's language or culture.
Both sound cold and uncaring, which is far from the spirit in which
Ignatius used them. A better word might be *balance*.

In his *First Principle and Foundation,* Ignatius talks about "making
use of those things that help to bring us closer to God and leaving aside
those things that don't."

At first this notion seemed rather exploitative to me, as if the whole
of creation were only there for us to select from it the bits that seem to
serve our purpose. It didn't come to life for me until one day when I was
sitting on a bench in a quiet, sunny courtyard, looking at a fuchsia
bush. It was late August, and the bees were constantly visiting the fuchsia. They would land very gently on those flowers that were fully open
to receive them. They made no attempt to enter a closed flower or to
force the petals in any way. When they found an open flower they crept
into its depths to extract the nectar. In doing so, of course, they also carried the pollen from flower to flower, bush to bush, thus ensuring further fruitfulness.

As I watched them, I realized that although the bees were choosing
the fuchsia flowers and disregarding other plants growing in the courtyard, other insects were seeking their nourishment from different
sources. In choosing what was exactly right for them, they were not only
receiving their own nourishment but were also playing an essential role
in the fruitfulness of their environment. And in choosing one plant
rather than another, they were in no way rejecting or denigrating the
others. The secret of this harmonious, cooperative life seemed to lie in
each creature's being true to its own essential nature. Each gained what

it needed for survival and growth from the source that was right for it, and it did so without harm either to itself or to the flowers. In fact, after each encounter, both insect and flower were left in a richer state than before: the insect had been nourished and the flower had been pollinated.

I found this picture to be a very vivid illustration of what it might mean to "make use of what leads to life" and to leave aside what, for each individual, does not lead to life. It was a truly creative kind of "detachment." It helped me to understand what God might be calling us to when he asks us to let go of our attachments. The bees, I noticed, made no attempt to "possess" the flowers, nor did the flowers attempt to trap and hold the bees. This was a free interchange, perfectly fulfilling the needs of the bees, the fuchsia, and the wider circle of creation around them.

The game of Monopoly gives us another example of where excessive attachment can lead. If one player buys up all the hotels and utilities and amasses more and more property, the game ceases to flow because the other players have less and less, and eventually the whole thing seizes up. In a more sinister way, we see such patterns at work in the way we manage our economies and our international dealings.

We are led back to the first question again: Whose kingdom am I serving, my own or God's? It takes a lot of courage to recognize the truth that we ourselves are not the fixed center of things but rather that we are beings through whom life flows. But when we do understand and acknowledge this, we discover that our emptiness will lead us more surely to our true purpose than our imagined fullness ever could, because God's life and grace will flow so much more fully and freely through empty hands.

Instinctively, however, we step back from the brink of the flow. For most of us, most of the time, the main thrust of our energy is spent in building and maintaining our "riverbank homes"—those things that make us feel secure and important: our jobs, our possessions, our ambitions. We construct a little world around ourselves that feels permanent and solid. Of course, in our humanity, we need to feel safe and solid; it's part of how God made us. But only part. There is another dimension of our being—perhaps, we might say, the eternal reality of who we are—which is not at home on the riverbank but is longing for the flow of the river itself.

Letting go of our riverbank dependencies will be painful and may even seem impossible, as we began to see in the last chapter. If you could ask a newborn baby how it would survive without the placental food, it would answer, "Impossible." But the midwife knows better. God is our midwife through all the trauma and the joy of our coming-to-birth in him—and God is gentle. . . .

> The journey with God does not deny our natural needs and desires, but it rearranges our priorities and nudges us constantly with the call forward, as surely as the ocean draws the rivers. Our attachments begin to look like riverbank constructions that tempt us to get out onto dry land and stay there, where it seems so comfortable, desirable, and safe. But if we do, there will be no on-flowing for us, no on-growing, no progress toward the full freedom of the children of God.

Dealing with Our Addictions

An infallible cure for a headache is to drop a rock on your toe! I have tried this, accidentally, in practice, and I know that it works. I may have been totally obsessed by my headache; it might have been flooding my entire consciousness to the exclusion of everything else, but as soon as I felt the effects of the rock on my foot, my obsessive attention to the headache was immediately mollified. It is human nature to focus our attention on the matter that most powerfully engages our feelings, whether the feelings are of pain or pleasure, fear or desire.

The purpose of this chapter is to look at those things in our lives that are having the "headache effect" in that they are taking over our consciousness and filling us up in ways that may be blocking the flow of grace and life. We tend to think of addictions as serious chemical dependencies, as with alcohol or drugs. But an addiction is perhaps more helpfully defined as a program of dependency, often on things that are harmless in themselves, that has become "hardwired" in us to the extent that it determines our whole way of behaving and relating to each other. At this point in our journey, therefore, we ask God to reveal our addictions to us, because he comes to free us from captivity and begins by showing us where the knots are in the ropes that bind us.

A Skating Lesson

Another example may help. I have never learned to ice skate, but I have always admired those who can and have thought how wonderful it must be to glide confidently across the rink to the rhythm of the music. If we imagine ourselves on the ice rink, we can grasp something of the difference between addiction and freedom. At first we cling with both hands to the rail, gingerly edging our way around. The process is tedious and lumbering, a million miles removed from the lightness and joy of movement in the middle of the rink where the real skaters are. There seems to be an unbridgeable gulf between ourselves and them.

The learning process goes on. Perhaps we find ourselves able to let go of the rail with one hand and move painfully forward instead of sideways like a crab. Yet the dominant feeling is still one of fear, of falling and making fools of ourselves. What might bring about a transformation from this fear-ridden rail-clinging to the joy of the ice dance?

Suppose that we were able to put aside our dominant experience of fear and allow ourselves instead to be taken over by the music. Let's try it in our imagination. You have nothing to lose—you are on solid ground, and you are not about to break a leg. Let the music take you over. Imagine it flowing through your ears all the way down to your feet. See where it leads them. Watch as it leads them off into the middle of the ice. Don't just watch. Go with them! They are surer guides to your deepest desire than your fear-logged head! What, after all, is your deepest desire in this exercise? To stay with the safety of the rail or to experience the joy of the dance? You can't have both. You have to choose!

All very well, you may say, but this has little to do with my lived experience. True, most of us are not likely to be much of a challenge to Torvill and Dean, but the same principles apply in our struggles against all the addictions, great and small, that impede our inner journey. The secret of transformation has to do with where our energy is really flowing. Is it staying with the fear or being tempted by the joy? In more general terms, are we dwelling on the negative feelings and reactions in ourselves, or are we directing our energies toward the positive feelings?

Do we more often ask ourselves, "How do I stop doing this bad thing?" or "How can I find more time and energy for this good thing?

Two phrases that we might take to heart as warning signals are *if only* and *what if.* The if onlys of our life give us an excuse for dwelling on the past and on the unchangeable features of our circumstances: "If only I'd worked harder at school, lived in a different country, had a different set of genes, had more tolerant parents. . . . The what ifs have the same negative effects in the future tense: "I'd like to try, but what if . . . I should fail, my friends think I'm being silly, I lose my job," etc. The thing about if onlys and what ifs is that we will never know how things might have been, if . . . or how things will possibly work out, if . . . so energy spent on them is definitely negative energy that is not leading us closer to God but is pulling us down more deeply into a spiral of desolation.

Sink or Swim?

I discovered another picture of freedom one night while lying in a warm, deep bath. I had emptied one of the little plastic bottles of bath oil into the water, hoping that its promise to be "revitalizing" would rouse me from the threat of lethargy and despondency that was lurking around the corner.

I watched idly as the bottle bobbed up and down on the water. Then I held it down and filled it up. I let it go and watched it sink slowly down and settle on the bottom. I fetched it up again, emptied it, and let it float. My childish pastime made me realize that God sometimes does the same with me. I fill up, gradually, with all the things I desire and want to hold on to. The more I fill up, the deeper I sink, until eventually I lie like a lead balloon at the bottom of the bath, quite incapable of movement. Then something happens to "tip me up and pour me out." It is usually something unwelcome that I resist with all my strength, but if it succeeds in draining me of all the attachment feelings I have collected, then something new happens. The little bottle bobs up again, freed of its cargo of bathwater, light, floating, and responding to every wave. This is the gift of emptiness; only in my emptiness can I be sustained by the buoyancy of God's unfailing love and move on as he created me to in order to grow.

Using the Stick, or Scenting the Carrot?

As we have been discovering, with Ignatius, the truth is often blindingly simple and obvious. The deepest desire leads most surely to God. Just as the pain in my foot was greater than the ache in my head and I therefore diverted my energy from my headache to my injured foot, so, too, the magnetic power of the music and the desire to dance on the ice will override my fear of falling and letting go.

God teaches us like the children we are. He uses carrots, not sticks. He attracts us through our own deepest desires and not through threats of eternal punishment. He calls us to the joy of his presence by inviting us to discover, in our own deepest desires, his own overwhelming and passionate desire for us. What does this tell us about how to deal with our addictions? Two possible strategies suggest themselves.

There is a way that we might call the *stick way* (or the *ascetic way*). This strategy says something like this:

- I am becoming aware that I have these particular dependencies, attachments, compulsions, crutches, idols (or whatever you may like to call them).
- I will spend all my energy in trying to destroy them.
- If my idols are like the golden calf of the Israelites, then I will attend to the matter of getting rid of my calf.
- I will achieve freedom in this way.

The second way might be called the *carrot way* (or the *way of deepest desire*). This strategy says:

- I am becoming aware that I have these particular dependencies, attachments, compulsions, crutches, idols, etc.
- I will not try to get rid of them by my own efforts.

- Instead, I will use the limited energy I have to attend to those things in my experience where I feel right with God, or on solid ground, or living true.
- These will become the music in my heart that leads me into the dance and overrides the fear that keeps me clinging to the rails.
- I will not spend my energy trying to melt down my golden calf.
- Instead, I will turn my attention to the holy mountain and my journey toward it, with all of God's surprises along the way.
- In this way God will lead me to freedom without my even realizing that it is happening.

We can notice significant differences between these two strategies:

- The first is me centered; the second is God centered.
- The first is labored and heavy; the second is light and joy filled.
- The first depends on sticks, the second on carrots.
- The first is centered on my fears, the second on my desires.
- The first is a burden, the second an adventure.

As a practical exercise, we might try noticing those things in our immediate experience that are operating by the stick method and those that are reflecting the way of the carrot. Which things, for example, are draining us of energy, and which are generating new energy in us? Are we in the habit of using the stick on ourselves more than we follow the carrot?

The Promise of the Garden

When Mary Magdalene met Jesus in the resurrection garden, he warned her not to cling to him. Take time to reflect on that scene for a moment. . . . Mary thinks she really knows Jesus, and she has staked her whole life on that knowledge. Small wonder that, out of the grief of Calvary, she clings with joy to what appears to be a return to *how things were.*

Jesus won't let her do this because he is calling her forward to *how things will be.* He knows that she can never be free to move on with him to this wholly new and unimagined reality as long as she clings to her dependency on the limited realities of what she has known so far. He loves her enough to cut her free from her riverbank certainties and draw her with him into the flow of life.

In that brief but timeless encounter, Mary, and we along with her, moves forward from the frightened person who seeks to hold on to what she so fears to lose, to the confident and empowered apostle who leaves the garden to become the channel for the first flow of the post-resurrection gospel. Mary, and we, are born into a whole new dimension of freedom because Jesus has cut the cord of our former needs and dependencies and launched us into the promised fullness of life-in-him.

Stepping-Stones

You might like to reflect on the following prayer picture. If it helps you, then use it to lead you into your own prayer. If not, then, like the bees in the bushes, leave it aside.

"Each breath a stepping-stone to God."

These words have made a home in my heart. I let the feeling paint its picture in my prayer today. I let myself walk into the picture, feel the swirl of the river, and stand on the stepping-stone. My whole prayer today wants to be just time standing there in God's unseen presence, on the stepping-stone.

The river is wide, so wide that I can't see the other shore, however hard I strain my eyes. The water is clear and wild, full of unseen currents and unexpected rapids but calm shallows as well. I feel at home in the river, standing on an island of truth.

Behind me on the riverbank is my little home, a stone-built cottage that keeps me warm and safe and keeps the world at bay. My cottage is my kingdom, a place to return to when the river runs too wild and too cold, or when predators stalk the shoreline.

There is something disconcerting in the view out over the water. What had seemed like a journey of adventure when I began to seek God's truth and his Kingdom, is not all that it seemed because I can see only one stepping-stone, and I'm standing on it. There is no way forward.

I can't do anything about my position. I'm standing here in the water on the one and only stone. All I can do is stand here in the present moment and realize that there is no journey because there is no way. There is a line of stones left behind me, but I don't want to go back. Truly, I don't want to go back.

For a moment I feel a wave of panic, but it recedes and leaves me free to stand on my stone, breathing the air, feeling the spray of the water, listening to God's heartbeat pulsing through creation. And waiting, just waiting, for God.

And then, when my heart is still, God is there beside me, silently placing the next stone in front of me and inviting me to take another step into the trackless waters. Another breath, another prayer, another stone. Just one more stone.

My breathing becomes steady, each breath a stepping-stone to God. As time passes, I learn to recognize God's ways, and to trust, when I stand in the middle of the fast-moving water, that he will always bring me one more stone—just one—and call me forward to one next step. I welcome his arrival, and smile my silent greeting.

I come to expect him and to know I can rely on him. I stand here on my stone, my little rocky island, and feel a ripple of anticipation as I turn toward the riverbank to greet him as he comes. He is a little late today, still there on the riverbank searching out the right stone. And only now I see how he is doing it. He is taking the stones away, one by one, from my cottage on the riverbank. Already it is half demolished. He is dismantling my kingdom, bit by bit, to provide me with the way to discover his.

SUGGESTIONS FOR PRAYER AND REFLECTION 10

The Parable of the Weeds

[Jesus] put another parable before them, "The kingdom of heaven may be compared to a man who sowed good seed in his field. While everybody was asleep his enemy

*came, sowed darnel all among the wheat, and made off. When the new wheat
sprouted and ripened, the darnel appeared as well. The owner's servants went to
him and said, 'Sir, was it not good seed that you sowed in your field? If so, where
does the darnel come from?' 'Some enemy has done this,' he answered. And the
servants said, 'Do you want us to go and weed it out?' But he said, 'No, because
when you weed out the darnel you might pull up the wheat with it. Let them both
grow till the harvest; and at harvest time I shall say to the reapers: First collect the
darnel and tie it in bundles to be burned, then gather the wheat into my barn.'"*

(Matthew 13:24–30)

LET THE LORD speak to you through this parable about the weeds and
the good seed growing in the field of your own heart. You might feel
drawn to ask him what to do about your own weeds (attachments) and
listen to his guidance to you. Then ask him to show you the infinite
value of the crop that is growing in you.

IF YOU CAN imagine your life as a river between its riverbanks, in what
ways do you feel tempted to build "riverbank houses" for yourself?
Where do you feel more comfortable—on the bank or in the flow? Can
you see what draws and holds you to the riverbank and what attracts
you onward in the flow?

IS THERE SOMETHING that you would really love to do in your life but
about which you don't yet have the courage to "let go of the rails"? Bring
your fear honestly before God in your prayer, and then let him direct
your gaze toward your desire. Which has the stronger pull: your fear
or your desire? Do you want things to stay the way they are, or would
you welcome change and transformation? Lay your feelings before God,
without disguises or excuses.

CAN YOU RECALL a time when you have felt "tipped up and poured
out"? Now, with hindsight, would you say that this experience was, in

the longer term, deadening or enlivening? Did it diminish or increase your inner freedom?

LOOK CRITICALLY at an attachment that perhaps you very much wish you didn't have. How are you dealing with it now — using a stick or a carrot? Is your method effective? If not, what would you wish to do in order to change it? Bring your desire for change to God in your prayer and ask for the grace to refocus your energy.

HAVE YOU EVER in your life felt cut off from something or someone you thought was essential to your well-being? If so, recall in prayer the longing you felt to return to how things were. Since that time, your future has unfolded itself a little more. Do you still feel the same sense of loss and desperation, or has your experience moved you forward at all toward how things shall be?

YOU MIGHT LIKE to meditate on Mary Magdalene's meeting with Jesus in the resurrection garden (John 20:11–18). Show the Lord your tears and your grief, as she did. Hear the words "Do not cling. . . ." Let Jesus touch your pain and infuse you with the power and the confidence of his liberating love for you, his unfailing faith in you.

11

RECOGNIZING THE ENEMY,
TRUSTING THE FRIEND

BEFORE WE LOOK at the big questions around the promises and challenges of inner truth and inner freedom, I'd like to share a dream with you, one that left me with a useful picture of what can happen when we are "hooked."

In my dream, I was traveling in a train. Before we had traveled far, the driver himself came to visit me and showed me the map of our journey. I didn't know the places we would pass through—they were all part of an unknown future that didn't mean anything to me—but the driver traced the route on the map with his finger, smiled at me, and commented: "We will be traveling due north throughout the whole journey."

We continued the journey and came to a station. It was a bewitchingly beautiful station, a cottage that had been converted. Its walls were covered in climbing plants and flowers, honeysuckle, clematis, fuchsia. Its little leaded windows were sunk deep in its solid, white-washed, sun-drenched walls. Along the platform, little tables were set out. Everything about the station invited the traveler to disembark, abandon the journey, and settle in this beautiful place.

However, in my dream I didn't disembark. I decided to stay with the journey. And after that decision the journey became noticeably less agreeable. I became aware that terrible things were happening, unseen, but guessed-at, on the train. Children were being killed; people were being ill-treated; prisoners were being transported. I became uneasy and fearful, but the evil, whatever it was, remained invisible.

My fears became explicit when I noticed someone hanging on a hook from the buffers between two empty freight cars. A cold shock wave ran through me as I realized how easily this person could be crushed between the cars or fall to his death on the rails below. But before I could do anything about it, a huge arm reached out from the top of one of the cars, and a thick, grasping hand took hold of the person, hauled him off the hook, dropped him into the cavernous, empty car, and left him there with no way of either survival or escape. This "evil arm" seemed to belong to a malignant presence that was part of the situation of the train, always traveling with it and wreaking havoc but not, significantly, ultimately in control of it. The evil presence, though vicious and powerful, was not the driver of the train.

The Strategy of Enslavement

I awoke from my dream, which had almost (but not quite) turned into a nightmare. It was time to reflect, as I knew that the dream had been important. Let me share those reflections, in the hope that you may find some resonance with your own experience. This is what my dream taught me:

- The train, which you might see as our journey with God, was on an unswerving course due north ("true north"). The driver's reassurance was more powerful than any of the evil that was being perpetrated aboard the train.
- The cottage converted into a station was so enticing that I was tempted to stay forever in that place. In fact, it had all the makings of an addiction—a hook. The word *conversion* was significant. Even our deepest conversion experiences, because they are so beautiful and so loaded with positive feelings, can become addictive, holding us bound to the signpost instead of journeying on to the destination.

- Evil is endemic in our world. It travels, invisible and insidious, on
  our journey, an ever present threat. It brings about every imagin-
  able destruction. But this invisible, intangible evil needs hands and
  feet, minds and hearts, to do its work. How does it enlist its troops?
- The "evil arm" plucks the "hooked" person down and drops him
  into the cavern of captivity. When I reflected on this moment in
  the dream, I realized a very simple, obvious truth:

Evil can get hold of me in the place where I am hooked. Like a fish
on a line, I am helpless to escape its grasp as long as I am hanging on
my hook. Wherever I am hooked, evil forces can (quite literally) do
whatever they like with me. The next stage, after addiction, is enslavement. My hooks are the entry points in my life for the negative, destructive movements. Once enslaved, I can so easily be forcibly enlisted
into the ranks of this false commander.

And so Satan goes on his fishing trips, day by day, plucking us from
our hooks as we might pluck an apple off a tree, because in that position we are powerless to defend ourselves. So subtle is the process that
we don't even see the risk; we don't even realize what is happening. And
he doesn't take us off the hook to release us but to enslave us, just as the
fisherman takes his catch off the hook and flings it into the dark bowels
of the boat, ready to be gutted and sold.

We needn't labor the point—it's enough to realize that this macabre
little tale illustrates, in a few short moments of dreaming, the strategy of
the negative forces that are ranged against us, roaming our hearts, continually looking for ways of becoming embodied in our lives and the
lives of our communities.

We can follow up on this story, each in our own way. Once we are
enslaved by our specific compulsions, we find it increasingly easy to do
wrong in order to keep ourselves supplied with whatever it is we so
need (which could be something intangible, such as affirmation, popu-
larity, or power). Which of us has not, at some time, undermined a colleague for our own advancement, jeopardized a relationship to get our
own way, risked our health and safety or that of others to make a profit,
lied or cheated to maintain our image? Which of us has not allowed

some addictive habit to become embodied in our character, distorting and polluting the whole way we live, feel, and act, until, like a cancer, the habit runs out of control and starts to take us over?

And the Strategy of Liberation?

On the face of it, liberation doesn't sound very inviting. It is about all those things that keep us hooked and about all the agony of coming off the hooks. As we have noticed in our own painful experience, getting unhooked can be devastating. It feels like losing so much of what we most value. Freedom is costly—we pay with the currency of our hearts. The difference, when we surrender to the liberator, is that we are asked to choose our own destiny rather than remain puppet slaves of our compulsions. In my dream, this choice was reflected in the decision not to settle in the beautiful station but to risk the onward journey. This was also a choice between a deep desire (to stay in the beautiful place) and an even deeper desire (to travel on). The choice I made was a reflection of my own deepest desiring.

At the moment of choosing, the options seemed unequal. The immediate fascination of the station looked far more attractive than the rigors of the journey still to come. So why did I opt for the journey? Surely because my deepest desire was to reach the longed-for destination (true north!), and this desire was stronger than the desire to stay in the place of consolation, and strong enough to help me through the barriers of difficulty along the way. The strategy of liberation seems to work something like this:

- I start to realize that everything I have—including my time, my talents, my feelings, my circumstances, and even those things I am hooked on—are all gifts.

- I don't have — and can't have (by the nature of things)—any permanent hold on anything because I myself am only passing through the created world at this moment in time, and everything else is equally transient. To try to hold on to things (or people) is to reverse the natural logic of creation and set myself up as creator.

- Because nothing is mine in any real or permanent way, I have (ultimately) nothing to fear from apparent losses in my life, and (ultimately) nothing to gain from transient acquisitions or achievements — though of course it won't feel like this at the surface of myself. If I can begin to live from the free center where these things are really true for me, I become free of the constant need to hold on to what I fear to lose, or to strive neurotically after what I hope to gain. All the energy that has been needed to maintain this holding on and striving after becomes freed for the thrilling challenge of becoming who I really am.

- Paradoxically, this doesn't diminish my delight in creation and all its gifts: quite the opposite. I find, when I stop seeing other things and other people primarily as contributors to my own well-being, and through the blinders of how I can obtain them or keep them, or even get rid of them, that my whole vision widens out. I begin to see these objects or people *as they really are:* quite separate and other from me, and pregnant with their own mystery. It's as if a distorting filter has been removed from the lenses of my vision. People are no longer defined for me by my own subjective desires or fears but by their own objective reality. I am free to enter into true relationship with them, and they with me. One thread in the tapestry of life has been redeemed.

The fictitious story below may help to illustrate this process.

Christine was the mother of a teenage son, Derek. As he came closer to the age when he would leave home, she became increasingly obsessed with keeping him close to her. Her great fear of losing him stemmed from her fear of the loneliness that would invade her life when he was no longer living at home. This fear was becoming her main motivator.

It followed that she began to see everything that Derek did or said in terms of this deep-seated fear. If Derek had a girlfriend, Christine feared losing his love. If he showed interest in a course away from home, she feared losing contact with him. If they argued, she feared losing his goodwill. She was hooked to her need of her son.

To keep herself supplied with what she thought she needed, she began to use manipulative behavior. She started to criticize his friends and invent stories against them. She started to "lose" any mail that came to him from colleges away from home. She became ill when he wanted to go away for the weekend. She gave in to his every whim, for fear of upsetting him. Their whole relationship became unbalanced.

It's not difficult to see the pattern of enslavement in this: First Christine becomes hooked to her need-love for Derek. She builds her life upon the false assumption that he is hers and that she can hold on to him. To keep herself supplied with this false need-love, she begins to do actual harm, interfering with his freedom and slandering his friends.

While she hangs on this hook, she is easy prey for the life-destroying, enslaving spirit that we might call Satan. He plucks her off and drops her into the slavery wagon, where her whole life becomes a cage devoted to retaining her hold on her son. Satan has won the day. The possibility of a real and free love between mother and son is destroyed . . . unless the liberating power can be allowed entry into the situation.

Now see how the strategy of freedom might reverse this process:

Derek makes up his mind to fly the nest and takes up study at a distant university. Christine is devastated. They have a massive row, and Derek leaves home. Christine's hook has come out of the ceiling and she is lying, so to speak, in a crumpled heap on a cold, hard floor.

For the first time, she comes face-to-face with the reality that her son is not hers to possess. This knowledge is bitterly painful, but it is potentially life-giving. It is a Calvary moment. All her efforts to hold on to Derek, she now realizes, were a futile waste of energy. She lets go of them.

After some weeks the first shock has subsided. She phones Derek and suggests a visit. Slightly reluctantly, he agrees, and they fix a date for her to visit him in his new home. She begins to direct her energies into planning the visit. As she does so, she remembers moments from his childhood, and the happy memories give rise to a feeling of genuine gratitude for the times they have enjoyed. The store of memories becomes a source of renewed energy for her.

When the weekend of the visit arrives, she sees her son in a rather different light. Now he is an independent young man, with a group of interesting friends and a vision of his own future. She is surprised to find how much he has changed!

In fact, of course, it is Christine who has changed—or, more correctly, her way of seeing her relationship with Derek has changed. Without the distorting filters of her need-love, she is free now to see him and relate to him as he really is, a separate and independent human being, full of his own mystery, and a delight to be with.

Meanwhile, back home, now forced to face the lonely life she once dreaded, she is beginning to use her energies to discover new interests in a lifestyle that is opening up more opportunities than she had ever imagined possible.

And if we take this logic of enslavement and liberation into some of the political and social issues of our time, we will find much more dramatic examples of the insidious power of evil to infiltrate our relating and decision making, and of the hard cost, but rich reward, of surrendering to the way of freedom.

Watch Out for the Devil in Disguise!

Jesus warned us that other shepherds would appear who would, in truth, be wolves in sheep's clothing. Mostly we think of these false guides as being external to ourselves, as indeed they may be, in the form of manipulative leaders or those who turn the spreading of God's Word into a multimillion-dollar enterprise in which they are the chief shareholders.

Ignatius, however, warns us of a different kind of threat from the false spirits. We have already seen how they are present in the destructive inner movements that lead us toward desolation and hence, away from God. Even more dangerously, they can be operating in what appears to be consolation. Here is an example.

Over a number of days my prayer had been centered on the events of Jesus' suffering and death, and the prayer had been very fruitful, showing me several aspects of my own life and journey that needed

God's healing and my attention. I began to realize, however, that I was somehow resisting crossing the threshold from Friday to Sunday and taking my prayer forward to the resurrection. Eventually I did move on and tried to bring myself to the scene in the garden where Mary Magdalene meets the risen Lord. Imagine my reaction, therefore, after all this hesitation, when I "saw" Jesus there in my prayer, holding up a hand to prevent my coming nearer, and saying, in quite a forbidding tone, "Don't touch!" The prayer left me feeling desolated and distressed. I decided then and there that I wouldn't go back to that scene in prayer, and indeed, that for a while at least I wouldn't pray at all! All this happened in the small hours of a tearful night. (This is a typical example of changing course during desolation and reneging on decisions taken during consolation!)

It happened that the next day I was going to spend the weekend with a friend with whom I am on the same wavelength. Some time into the visit, I felt able to tell her about the "Don't touch!" prayer and how I felt about it. She listened quietly; then she spoke a wise word to me: "Do you think that these effects were really from God?" she asked. At first I was so sure that it was Jesus I had encountered in my prayer and that those hard words "Don't touch!" had been genuinely addressed to me and pointed to something I needed to look at. But as I reflected on my friend's words, I realized that the aftereffects—desolation and distress and a desire to abandon prayer—were actually the mark of a negative movement, or what Ignatius would call the false spirits.

This was an example, I believe, of what Ignatius calls "Satan appearing as an angel of light," or, in more contemporary terms, of a negative movement in my heart infiltrating my prayer in a way that seemed to be wholly the positive experience of an encounter with God in prayer. In fact, the apparently harsh attitude of Jesus was really a manifestation of my own psyche, projecting my own anxieties onto Jesus in a way that was unhelpful to our relationship.

When this happens, it isn't always easy to recognize it. One test is to look at the aftereffects of the experience and see whether they are leading you toward God or away from him. Another sound guideline is to share your experience and your reactions with a trusted friend or spiritual director, who will be able to reflect back to you the way the experience seems to have been working on you. This can be particularly helpful because, as you can see in my own example, when you are in the grip of this kind of negative movement, which appears to be so positive, you can be blind to the effects of your prayer and completely fail to register the obvious fact that these desolating feelings are not coming from God.

It doesn't follow, though, that the fact that something hard and challenging comes up in prayer means that it is not coming from God. It wasn't the apparently hard words in the prayer that showed that it was not from God—it was the effect of the prayer on me. Suppose that the same words, in the same prayer, had left me feeling a desire to go back to God and ask him to take me deeper into their meaning for me. There might still have been tears, but they would have been tears of consolation rather than the sobs of desolation. If these had been the aftereffects, then discernment would have suggested that this prayer was indeed rooted in God. In this example, the effect of wanting to abandon prayer was the most telling clue to the nondivine origin of this inner movement. It was also a clear case for applying the "Act against It" rule. People who are in a deep and loving relationship with God and have been practicing discernment for years are often easy prey to this particular manifestation of negative movements. Therefore, beware!

When the Fog Lifts

Some years ago, an elderly relative, Max, came to spend a few weeks' holiday with us. It was a wonderful autumn that year, and the trees were a joy to behold. Max seemed to enjoy his stay, but he had a strong attachment to his clothes, which meant that if they were to be laundered during his stay, we would have to sneak them away by night and have them dried again by morning. This coping mechanism functioned well, but we hadn't thought of extending it to his glasses.

Then, one particularly lovely clear morning he remarked, "I do like it here, but is it always so foggy?" It wasn't easy to convince him that the fog had its origins not in the external world but in the layer of grime on his glasses.

The nature of the difficulty rings bells in my own experience—perhaps in yours, too? I know that I can bring huge amounts of energy to bear on the task of convincing myself and others that the outside world is where the problem is, and that the lenses of my own vision are immaculately clear! It can be mortifying when circumstances remove our spectacles and submit them to a humiliating cleansing. But the view thereafter is breathtaking!

SUGGESTIONS FOR PRAYER AND REFLECTION   11

I tell you most solemnly,

I am the gate of the sheepfold.

All others who have come

are thieves and brigands;

but the sheep took no notice of them.

I am the gate.

Anyone who enters through me will be safe:

he will go freely in and out

and be sure of finding pasture.

The thief comes

only to steal and kill and destroy.

I have come

so that they may have life

and have it to the full.

I am the good shepherd:

the good shepherd is one who lays down his life for his sheep.

The hired man, since he is not the shepherd

and the sheep do not belong to him,

abandons the sheep and runs away

as soon as he sees a wolf coming,

and then the wolf attacks and scatters the sheep;

this is because he is only a hired man

and has no concern for the sheep.

I am the good shepherd;

I know my own

and my own know me.   (John 10:7–14)

CENTER YOURSELF into stillness of heart in whatever way is helpful to you, and try to recall a time or situation in your own life when you felt frightened and unguided in a dark, stormy night. You may even be feeling like this right now.

Read the passage slowly, as often as you feel drawn to do so.

In your prayer, listen with all your being for the call of the shepherd, coming to you through the storm. There is so much noise in the night, and your eyes are so blind in the dark. How will you know that the call you are hearing is the shepherd's call, and not some attacker pretending to be the shepherd?

Use your memory to recall how the shepherd's voice has come to you in other situations in which you felt lost and threatened. Listen for those same tones now.

Out of all the clamor of the night, the shepherd's call rings clear and true to your heart: how do you feel now?

As you recall or imagine this situation, ask yourself this one question: did you find the shepherd, or did the shepherd find you?

TRY WATCHING an evening of television and reflect on one or two specific commercials. What signals are the advertisers giving us about our needs and desires? In what ways are they manipulating our anxieties and doubts about ourselves? Do you think that they are operating a strategy of enslavement or of liberation?

A way to check this out might be to ask this question: Am I being encouraged to claim something as my own and reap some advantage from that possession, or am I being invited to let go of something and trust that in doing so I shall be expanded rather than diminished?

You might like to take this kind of reflection a step further and apply similar questions to the way you see the Church operating. Is it, in your experience, bribing you with rewards, threatening you with punishments,

Can you name a personal hook in your life that is making you easy prey to the negative movements in your heart? In your prayer, simply lay the facts before God, and ask him to free you. In doing this, you will also be laying the facts open to yourself, and this in itself will move you beyond the stage of denying the problem.

or truly accompanying you on your journey to truth? Is it facilitating your freedom or colluding with your enslavement? If you feel uneasy with what you find in such reflection, how might you begin to change it, bearing in mind that we are the Church?

CAN YOU IDENTIFY any times or situations when you have come up against a false guide, either external to yourself or inside your own heart? What makes you feel that this guide was false? What tricks did this false guide use to try to seduce you into desolation and away from your true north?

RECALL ANYTHING that you have done or allowed to happen in the course of your life of which you are ashamed. Don't judge yourself; just try to trace back to the roots of the wrong action and identify the hook that first began the downward spiral into this situation. If you feel you have since been freed of that hook, thank God for your liberation. If not, lay it before him in prayer, and ask him to lead you closer to freedom.

CHILDREN BRING nothing into the world, and they know their own powerlessness. If you have a chance to watch a young child's response to Christmas, try noticing whether he is still receptive to everything as a gift, or whether he is already making demands and claims from a desire to possess. At what age does the child in your life seem to be passing from the first stage to the second? What might this tell us about Jesus' urging us to become as little children? Now reflect on your own response to seasons of gifting.

12 ◉

WHAT IS FREEDOM? WHAT IS TRUTH?

PILATE ASKED this second question of Jesus at the very point when Jesus had freely set aside his own freedom and allowed himself to be taken captive. Can you imagine the scene—the courtroom tension, the Passover, the excitement, the dawning knowledge in this man Pilate that there is something altogether different about the prisoner standing in front of him? Listen to his diversion tactics as he asks the question "What *is* truth?" in an effort to shift the focus of energy in the room away from himself and his deep unease about what he is getting into. Have you ever done that yourself when a conversation got too close to the mark, by diverting attention into some vague question that is safe precisely because it is so large and unanswerable?

But if we listen to the undercurrents in the courtroom, we may sense that these are not diversion tactics at all, but rather the first shaft of reality dawning in Pilate's heart, coming up spontaneously from the depths of his being. He is desperately seeking an answer out of the infinite space between himself and this condemned man whose life hangs on Pilate's choice. Hear that moment when the clarity of his heart-need speaks above the clamor in his brain:

"What *is* truth?"

When I was first thinking about the kinds of questions this book addresses, the question about freedom and truth seemed absolutely central. I had been confronted with Pilate's question myself, in an inescapable way, while praying the Passion and living out those Pilate tensions in my own heart. The question Pilate addressed to Jesus seemed to come rolling down the staircase of the centuries, bouncing and echoing on every step, until it came to rest by my own feet and demanded an answer. My way forward with the Lord seemed to depend on my picking this question up and letting it hang there in the space that separates me from God.

Yet the more I have thought about it, the more preposterous it seems to me even to suggest that these huge questions can in any sense be answered. So all I can do today is to share with you one or two pointers that have brought some light for me, living as I do in the gap between my falsehood and God's truth, between my captivity and the freedom into which I know God is drawing me.

When I hear Pilate's question echoing in my prayer, I know, increasingly, why it is so important. My old school had the Gospel words interpreted by Chaucer as its motto:

"And trouthe shal set thee free."

I lived with them for some years, emblazoned on my uniform and resounding out of every end-of-term assembly when we sang the school song. Gradually they insinuated themselves into my heart and sat there like an egg waiting for fertilization. It took over thirty years for that egg to come to ripeness, but when that finally happened, it took on a life of its own, as eggs do.

I knew all this when I began to think about these questions, and I knew, too, how central they are to any exploration of our inner landscape. But it was a bleak November evening when something clicked into place that helped me to take hold of the scale of the question, and it had to do with the matter of the *gap*. Let me explain.

Living in the Gap

The words that triggered my understanding that evening would
have seemed trite, had they not been spoken by someone who had obviously found them in the depths of his own experience.

God comes to us, he said

- not where we *should* have been if we had made all the right choices
  in life,
- not where we *could* have been if we had taken every opportunity
  that God has offered us,
- not where we *wish* we were if we didn't have to be in the place
  where we find ourselves,
- not where we *think* we are because our minds are out of sync with
  our hearts,
- not where *other people* think we are or think we ought to be when
  they are attending to their own agendas.

I had heard this kind of wisdom often enough before. That God meets
us *where we really are* is, after all, commonplace throughout our journeying. We all know that with our heads, but that evening I suddenly
grasped the truth of it with my heart, and that moment of truth brought
me a new degree of freedom—just as Jesus had said it would!

And, really, it was all about the gap.

I discovered that when I look at myself in any particular situation or
decision or meeting place with others, I see two points—you might
even call them *reference points*. One is the point where I really, truly am
before God. The other is the point from which I am in fact operating at
that moment. This really makes sense only if we look at some examples.

I'm in the office. My manager calls me in for my annual appraisal.
My next salary review depends on what is said in this meeting, so my career prospects hang on it. So does my self-confidence. He asks me,
"How do you see the job developing over the next three years?" Look at
two possible answers:

- "I hope to be leading a team in three years and taking on more responsibility."
- "I hope that in three years I'll be able to afford to get out of all this and do the things I really want to do with my life."

The first reply comes from the reference point set by where my manager thinks I am. I am telling him what I think he wants to hear. It isn't true. The second reply comes from where I really am. It expresses my truth, in this context, but I almost certainly won't say it out loud.

Sometimes the untrue response goes beyond words into action and life-changing decisions. Think, for example, of the young man who commits himself to an unwanted marriage because his teenage girlfriend is pregnant. He is operating from where he thinks he ought to be, but he will live for years to come in the tensions of the gap between who he truly is and the untrue place in which his decision has been made.

The heart of the problem doesn't lie so much in how we actually reply or what we actually choose to do, but in the tension between where we really feel drawn to be and where we are actually living out our days. The problem lies in this gap, but so does the solution. We begin to resolve this tension as soon as we acknowledge to ourselves and to God that it exists.

I'm sure you can multiply these examples, ad infinitum, from your own daily experience. Some seem almost too obvious to bother with— we all know these little dilemmas, and we learn to live with them. Others are potentially life shattering. So what struck me so forcibly that evening about the place where truth is?

I think it was disarmingly simple, really. I suddenly realized that wherever God is in all my lived experience, he is in the place where I really am, and not at any of these other false reference points that so often dictate my choices and decisions. For me, this was a quite amazing breakthrough. God is with me, wholly and lovingly present to me, at all those true places:

- the place where I recognize what I really prefer to do with my life,
- the place where I honestly acknowledge that what I am doing or deciding is at odds with my deepest desires,

- the place where I can say, "This is how I really feel," without the masks and defenses that I wear either to protect myself from other people, or to protect other people from the harsh stabs of my own true feelings.

Small wonder that I so often feel helpless and hopeless at the place from which I am trying to operate. It is not my true place. It is not the place where God is. And why isn't it the place where God is? Is not God in all things and at all places? Again, the answer seems too simple to register and yet profoundly true: God is not at our false reference points because God is truth, and he cannot be in falsehood. God is in the place where we truly are because that is where he is offering us his healing, his forgiveness, his strengthening, and his empowerment. There, and nowhere else, it seems to me, can we receive these gifts, and we reach our true place by becoming still before God and listening to his movements in our hearts.

A simple example illustrates the impossibility of meeting God other than at our true place, the place where we really are. I have a friend who is above-average height, who once confided in me that he wished God had made him a few inches shorter because nothing quite fits him. And another friend is below-average height, and I have no doubt that he sometimes wishes he could add a cubit to his stature. Yet if God were to speak to them where they wish they were instead of where they are, I'm guessing (physically speaking) they wouldn't hear him!

Much the same applies to our day-by-day actions and decisions. When we take them at the wrong place in our inner space—when we take them at a reference point that is not our truth—then we won't enjoy the liberating power of God-with-us in those actions and decisions. This is not because God is willfully withdrawing himself from us, but because he is truth, and our choices for falsehood, however excusable and understandable, can never be centered in him. They can never be true north, where our inner pendulum hangs straight. They will inevitably be affected by the movements that are pulling us out of plumb, out of balance.

> If we act from the true reference point of our Who center, a whole new source of energy breaks open inside us. This frees us to do the true thing from a place of power because this is the one place where our own desire is aligned with God's desire for us.

God, then, is with us where we really are, or where we are real, not at our false reference points. This may feel discouraging. After all, we do live much of our lives from these false reference points, but though God, who is truth, cannot be in falsehood, he can be, and is—I firmly believe from my own experience—in the gap! He is in the gaps that open up between where we truly are and where we pretend to be, wish to be, or think we ought to be. He is not only the truth, but also the *way*. When we meet Jesus in prayer and in our lived minutes, hours, and days, we are meeting the One who bridges the gap between our falsehood and his truth. Will we have the courage to walk across that bridge? The next chapter may help us to see how we might make the first step onto it by bringing our own experience into focus with the gospel experience in our prayer.

Noticing the Moment of Truth

If you develop the habit of listening carefully to other people's stories, you soon begin to notice those times when what they are sharing with you touches their heart truth. There will be a noticeable change in the energy level, indicated by their tone of voice or their body language generally. In some deep way, they come to life, they become energized, and you pick up the vibrations. Sometimes people can talk for hours—or, dare I say, live for years—without touching the truth in this way.

But eventually something is said or felt that causes them, inwardly, to change gears. It may bring them to tears, to laughter, to genuine self-disclosure in a conversation, or to a profound silence that you know marks holy ground. Perhaps a wall of stubborn resistance suddenly breaks down into a stream of tears that seems to flow from the person's deepest feelings. Or a controlled, courteous, correct conversation flares out into a flame of anger, setting free a long-harbored festering resentment for healing. This moment of truth, if it is grasped, can change the whole course of the person's response to the issue that is occupying him or her. It's as if some shell breaks open and a new way of being in the situation emerges, like a chick, with its own life and energy. But it takes courage to grasp the moment, and a sensitive companion can help enormously when such thresholds have to be crossed.

This makes it sound as if we live most of our lives entangled in a mesh of lies and falsehood. In a way, we do, and this is at the heart of our fallenness and our immense, immeasurable need of redemption. Not that we are consciously deceiving each other, or ourselves, in the big or small events and choices of our lives—it isn't that kind of deliberate sin. The web of falsehood holds us captive at a deeper level than consciousness. It slowly and insidiously programs us to operate from false reference points until we almost feel at home and comfortable in doing so.

This way of operating generates all kinds of complications in our relationships—a web of hidden agendas and defensive postures that are designed to conceal our reality and our truth rather than to help us to disclose ourselves in trust and love. When we stop to reflect that every person we meet carries his or her own personal entanglement through life, we can begin to see the true proportions of the problem and to glimpse the extent of our need of healing. This consciousness of the deep-rooted consequences of our fallenness—both global and personal—can be devastating, but it is the bedrock from which our journey to wholeness begins.

Because we are so inwardly blind, we feel almost comfortable in operating from false reference points. The word *almost* is significant. The problem with operating out of falsehood is that it always leaves us with a twinge (or perhaps even a surge) of spiritual desolation. In some way that we cannot articulate, our deepest desire—which has to do with being who we truly are—is being frustrated, and our hearts are registering their protest through feelings of turmoil and discontent. The way to healing begins when we learn to notice the moments of truth within ourselves and to respond to them by claiming the freedom they hold for us.

An Egg or an Orange?

> Untruth holds, ultimately, only death and disintegration, but truth carries life. In our moments of truth, something altogether new is set free.

I remember taking our young daughter one Christmas to a Christingle service. The children were all given a lovely ripe, succulent orange, decorated with the symbolic raisins and ribbon, and a candle as a sign of the Light of the World. It was a moving liturgy, and it wasn't until a week or so later, when the festivities were over and the orange was slowly withering, that it occurred to me how much truer a symbol of God's life in us, and ours in him, is the Easter egg than the Christmas orange. And now, as the memory floats back to me, I wonder whether the egg and the orange don't have something to tell us about truth and untruth.

Our untruths—our many false reference points—seem attractive and palatable and briefly satisfying. But as time passes, they start to rot. They may carry us over the awkward moment and briefly gain for us what we think we want. But they will not endure. They are like the house built on shifting sand that will ultimately not withstand the storm. They are not a place where God can make his dwelling.

Our truth, on the other hand, when we dare to name it and claim it, can feel like a raw egg—vulnerable, fragile and unpalatable—but (because it has been fertilized by God's Spirit in our hearts) it holds new life within it beyond anything we could hope for or imagine, and that new life has its own dynamic and carries its own new center of energy. Paradoxically, our raw egg becomes a rock-solid foundation for a life rooted in our truth center.

Claiming the Freedom

How might it feel, in practice, to observe our actions and reactions and reflect on whether they have their source in our truth or in one of our many falsehoods?

We have already noticed how, when we are really living true, we feel as if we were in touch with a source of energy far beyond our own. We have recalled, for example, the surge of energy we experienced when falling in love, engaging in some project or activity that drew deeply on our innate gifts, or becoming involved with something that moved us to active compassion or to a burst of creative expression.

To notice the difference between the limitations of our own energies and the power—and empowerment—that comes from the liberating energies of living true, compare the difference between cooking a routine meal for a picky, ungrateful child and preparing a special birthday cake as a token of love for her. Or consider the difference between stopping by the supermarket for the week's groceries and going to town to choose a gift for a loved one.

The difference hardly needs spelling out because we all know it from our own experience.

- When I do something out of duty, I need to muster all my energies to cope with the effort required. When I have done it, I feel drained. If I don't do it, I feel guilty. I am acting from a false reference point; I am acting from where I think I ought to be.
- When I do something out of love, I barely notice the demand on my energ—in fact, the action seems to generate new energy inside me, energy that I didn't know was there, and the task becomes almost effortless. I am acting from my true center, and the truth sets my creative energy free.
- The difference seems to lead us back to that question of desire. When my deeper desires are engaged, I have more energy, and I do what I do in a spirit of freedom. When my deeper desires are frustrated, I feel drained of energy, and I do what I do in a spirit of reluctance.

Only my truth is rooted in God. Those things in my life that spring from false reference points are like weeds that will fail to grow and bear fruit. Those things that spring from my truest center connect to a source of energy and power beyond myself, which frees my real potential.

When it comes to my deepest desire of all—my root desire that is leading me to my truest center—my energy level rises exponentially when that deepest desire is being nourished, but if it is being frustrated, the opposite will happen, and my vitality will be sapped and deadened. Like the Christingle orange, I will start to rot from the inside.

> *My deepest desire has to do with my sense of true north.*
>
> *When I feel that I am living true (however briefly), I am touching into my deepest desire.*
>
> *When I am living true to my deepest desire, I experience a new source of energy.*
>
> *This energy frees me and empowers me to live out my inner vision.*
>
> *This liberating empowerment is the action of the Holy Spirit in my heart.*

How then, do I claim freedom and energy? Simply, I think, by attending constantly to the inner compass that shows me when and where I am living true. By practicing discernment and nurturing the habit of living reflectively, each day I will notice where God has been acting in my lived experience. These are the moments of truth, and if I ask God to release the energy that is latent within them, I will begin to live out, in my daily tasks and relationships, the dream he has for me.

Freedom From or Freedom For

As early as the first chapter we noticed that there are two kinds of freedom:

- freedom *from* an oppressive or destructive situation, and
- freedom *for* a radically transformed way of being.

The first kind of freedom is something that we can strive for to free us from the addictions and compulsions that we looked at in chapters 9 and 10. This will benefit both ourselves and others, especially those who are less able to strive than we are, less strong, less empowered, less free.

The second kind of freedom lies at the heart of our desire for transformation. It is the journey to that center of ourselves, which, as we have seen, is indestructible. It is the source of our truth and our energy because it is the dwelling place of God.

Sometimes the first kind of freedom can lead us to the second. We struggle to become free of something that oppresses or diminishes us, and at first all our energy is focused on the desire for freedom *from*. But when that freedom has been won, either for ourselves or for others, the challenge to embrace the freedom *for* begins. We can see a vivid example of this in the struggle of the Eastern European countries in 1989 to free themselves from the oppression of state communism. Once the freedom was achieved, the much harder task of allowing that freedom to transform their societies began. Some responded to this new vocation. Others, like the Israelites freed from slavery in Egypt, wanted to turn back and revert to unfreedom with its apparently lower demands and lack of personal responsibility.

Perhaps a return visit to the circles of Where, How, and Who may help. Freedom from a destructive situation might be attempted, and sometimes achieved, by moving from one point on the Where circle to another, but that freedom for our eternal life in God is only found by moving into the Who center. We must carry all our unfreedom with us, allowing ourselves and our hurting and captivity to be touched by God at that center, and then we must move out again and carry the seeds of transformation back to the lived-out reality of our place in the Where.

You might like to reflect on what you find in your recent experience of these two different aspects of the call to freedom. What destructive or oppressive situations are you aware of within your own circumstances? Can you do anything about them?

Now, by contrast, reflect on your personal experience of the second kind of freedom. Have you been aware of any moments of truth in yourself when you knew you were living in accordance with your deepest desire? How did you respond? Were you aware of the release of new energy in yourself as a result of touching your heart-truth? How did you direct that energy? How did you live out the freedom that flowed from that encounter with truth?

Freedom Is Its Own Reward

Once, while I was on retreat (and therefore more prayerful and attentive than usual), I found myself reflecting on a particular situation in which I felt God was asking me to be more committed in cooperating with him in healing a damaged person. I wanted to say yes, but I knew that my consent would be costly to me and would involve risk and vulnerability. Then one morning, in prayer on a blustery hilltop among furze bushes, I heard some inner voice saying, *"I won't love you any more than I already do if you say yes, or any less if you say no."* My immediate reaction to this was to feel aggrieved. Surely, I thought, my commitment to doing God's will ought at least to bring me a few Brownie points on the salvation scale. But just as I was about to protest, the inner voice continued, *"Because to do so would be to violate your freedom."*

It was one of those moments when I knew beyond doubt that the truth that those words had expressed had freed me of all the complications surrounding the choice, had left me free to choose:

Without fear of loss
Without hope of gain

Perhaps for the first time in my life, at any conscious level, I knew what it felt like to make a free choice. It also made me realize how very few of my choices in life are genuinely made in freedom. I, and perhaps most of my fellow human beings, almost invariably make decisions that are influenced by our fear of losing something or our hope of gaining something. If you doubt this, read the papers critically, and see what is going on in Washington, for example. How many legislative decisions are made free of the fear of losing votes or the hope of gaining influence? Which of our leaders or politicians are, in general, operating from a position of inner freedom (there are some!)? Now bring the focus back to your own world. Recall some of the choices you have made today, this week, this year. When you made them, was your inner compass reading true north, or was it swinging out to one side or another?

For example, you may have chosen to visit someone. Did you make the visit because you were afraid the person would be offended if you didn't go? Or because he has a knack of making you feel important when you go? Or was the visit motivated solely by love?

I made my choice that day. In that particular matter I chose to say yes, but I chose freely, knowing that there was no reward offered, in the narrow sense. In that moment, I learned how it felt to choose in freedom, out of my own deepest truth. And in that free choice, I noticed how all the complications of negotiating my terms fell away, and how all the energy I had been using on those negotiations was released to fuel the task to which I had committed myself.

It also released in me a sense of peace, almost impossible to describe, that made me realize that the joy of living and acting from my true center (however intermittently) is truly the peace that passes understanding and the reality that satisfies my deepest desire. Even the journey of my heart home to God is not about the hope of some future heaven or fear of dark oblivion but simply the joy of each present moment lived fully in the freedom of a child of God.

I learned up on that hill what God had always known, that the freedom he was creating in my Who center was far more precious than any reward, and that my relationship with him and with every human friend and neighbor could grow and bear fruit only if it were rooted in that free center of truth, balance, and empowerment.

SUGGESTIONS FOR PRAYER AND REFLECTION   12

Jesus said, "I am the Way, the Truth and the Life.
No one can come to the Father except through me.
If you know me, you know my Father too."   (John 14:6 – 7)

RELAX, AND LET yourself be drawn deeply into the silence of your own heart. Hear Jesus saying these words to you personally.

Recall a situation when you know
you have acted out of your true center. Relive that situation in prayer.
What was said and done? How did
you feel? How did things work out?
Were you aware of any increased
flow of energy or sense of empowerment as a result?

Ask him to open your eyes to see—first
like a distant vision—the center of your own
truth, where he is indwelling.

Ask him, by the way of his cross, to make
a way—a causeway—between your many untruths, and your deepest center of truth in
him.

Ask him to set free in you the energy and
joy of his life, like a wellspring in your heart.

With this courage kindled in you, begin to make the journey from where
you feel you are, into your center of truth, watching as the distance
shortens and disappears.

LOOK BACK OVER the past few days or weeks. Have you found yourself
in any situation where you can see now, with hindsight, that you were
not operating from your center of truth but from some false reference
point? Take the situation into your prayer and reenact it. Reflect on
which reference point you were operating from; for example, was it
from where *someone else* expected you to be, from where you thought
you ought to be, from where you wish you were? Now, in the silence,
acknowledge your true reference point honestly and without fear to
God. He tells us that he is truth. Try to become aware of his presence in
your truth. However much you wish your feelings were not as they are,
become aware that God is precisely there in your true place, and that is
where he loves and accepts you unconditionally.

NEXT TIME YOU are engaged in a significant conversation, make a deliberate effort to notice where the threads of truth are running. In particular, notice moments when any of the participants (including
yourself) touches on a real moment of truth. What signs indicate that
truth has been touched (tone of voice, body language, depth of self-
disclosure)? Do you think the moment of truth is being acknowledged
and affirmed by other participants in the conversation? How might this
moment become life giving for the person concerned? For others?

WHICH TASKS THAT you have been doing today have drained you of energy, and which have appeared to recharge your batteries? What have you done out of a sense of duty, and what have you done for love? How does this difference relate to your own deepest desires? Which tasks have been in harmony with your personal inner vision?

IS THERE ANYTHING in your circumstances or relationships that you wish to be free of? Let your desire for freedom be laid open in your prayer. What kind of freedom are you seeking: freedom from something that exists in your life, or freedom for something new, or both? Do you feel that God is responding to your desire? Tell him, in your prayer, exactly how you are feeling.

RECALL TWO OR three major decisions that you have made in your life. As you look back on them, do you feel that you made your decisions out of fear of losing something, in the hope of gaining something, or quite freely?

13

To See You More Clearly

I T MAY SURPRISE and dismay you to learn that so far, three quarters of the way through these explorations, we have been occupied almost entirely with those aspects of the inner journey on which Ignatius invites retreatants to reflect during the First Week of the *Spiritual Exercises*. All the huge questions —

- about the deepest desire
- about addiction and detachment
- about truth and freedom
- about the realization that God's overwhelming love for us is the very ground of our being, preceding and superseding our own brokenness
- about realizing the scale of the mess we are in as well as the power and free availability of the redeeming love that alone can release us from it

— all these questions center on Ignatius's *First Principle and Foundation* and on his guidelines for learning to discern the inner movements of our hearts by recognizing consolation and desolation, by noticing when we are out of balance and when we are living true.

In any building designed to last, the foundation is the most important feature. On our estate is a house built on a site that turned out, when the first excavations were made, to be a former mine shaft. It doesn't take too much imagination to appreciate that more bricks and concrete went into building the foundation of that house than into its visible parts. The moral is obvious: the more unstable the ground, the deeper and firmer the foundation needs to be. For the great majority of us, the soil of our hearts, where God is making his dwelling place, is extremely unstable, which is why Ignatius, and we who learn from his wisdom, give so much attention to the foundations.

> Richard of Chichester's prayer ends "Day by day," reminding us that the *Exercises* are not an end but a beginning. The challenge of the journey is not to "make the *Exercises*" but to live the truth and the freedom into which God draws us, day by day, as we seek to see, to follow, and to love.

The prayer of Richard of Chichester, often associated with Ignatius, includes these three petitions:

To see you more clearly,
To love you more dearly,
To follow you more nearly,
Day by day.

This prayer is so simple that it trips off the lips of children in primary school, yet so far reaching that it can lead us to the very heart of God-with-us. The three petitions lead us, now, into the final chapters of our journey:

• to seek *to see the Lord more clearly,* by asking in prayer to become participants in the events and the teaching of his earthly life and ministry is the gift of the Second Week of the *Exercises,*

• to seek to *love the Lord more dearly,* by asking in prayer to be alongside him in his Passion and death and to share the joy of his resurrection are the gifts of the Third and Fourth Weeks of the *Exercises,*

• to seek *to follow the Lord more nearly,* by reflecting on what we can give *him* in response to the immensity of *his* love for *us* is a gift of the contemplation with which the *Exercises* end.

Intimacy with God

We have spent a lot of time exploring what we most truly desire and discovering those things that are getting in the way of the fulfillment of that desire. We begin this chapter by asking ourselves if it might be true to express at least part of our deep desire in this way:

I desire to know God better.

We can reflect on what happens in a human relationship as it grows and deepens. This happens when two people feel drawn to each other and then develop that feeling by revealing to each other something of who they most truly are. A relationship often begins with fairly generalized conversations where no risks are taken, as two people explore the "facts" about each other—where they live, what they do for a living, where they spend their vacations, etc. This may grow into a deeper exploration, based on questions more like: "Do you like your work?" "Do you wish you lived somewhere else?" "What makes you happy or sad?" And as the relationship grows and the two feel increasingly safe and at home with each other, more and more exposure can be risked. It even becomes possible to say, for example, "I really admire you, but you make me feel inadequate because . . ." or "I feel hurt because I don't understand why you said what you did." It may even become possible to take the greatest risk of all and say, "I love you."

Suppose the same dynamic were to apply in our relationship with God. We may begin our friendship with God in the no-risk statements that we learned as children and often express in our set prayers. Let's take some familiar words from the Lord's Prayer, "Thy will be done," and look at them in a deeper way.

We can chant these words almost like a mantra, rhyming them conveniently with "Thy kingdom come." We may have done that for years already, and we may continue to do so, in all faith and love, for the remainder of our lives. Such prayer has its own power.

Or we may load the words with a little more personal meaning: "I'm in a difficult position, Lord. I wonder what your will might be in all of this?"

Our desire to know God more intimately might invite us to greater risk taking: "I'm finding this so very hard, Lord. It goes against the grain, but I really, deeply want to do your will, and that desire is greater than my desire to do my own thing in this matter. Please help me."

Or the greatest risk of all: "Lord, I love you, and that's the mainstream of my life. Let your will and mine become one."

If you felt some resonance with the statement "I desire to know God better," then you are experiencing the call into deeper intimacy with him. If you respond to that call, he will draw you more deeply into friendship with him through your prayer and through everything in your lived experience. That friendship will develop by your revealing yourself more and more to him, and he to you, in a process of talking to and listening to each other, just as in human friendship.

Ignatius teaches us how to open ourselves up to this intimacy with God through Gospel-based meditation, through which we can, in our prayer, become participants in the life and ministry of Jesus and discover its reality for us where we are here and now.

Intimacy, whether with God or with another human being, challenges us to come closer, to take risks, to be open to change and transformation in a dynamic relationship that we cannot control. It engages us in:

- *listening*—by opening our hearts to God. We learn to become inwardly still and receptive to what God wants to show us,

- *disclosing*—revealing ourselves to God in prayer, just as we are,

- *sharing*—allowing the life of the Lord to become deeply connected to our own by absorbing his Word and by sharing in the events of his living, his dying, and his rising,

- *reflecting*—deepening our experience of God by becoming more and more aware of the ways in which he meets us in our daily lives,

- *giving*—freely offering to others the gifts we have received ourselves; sharing God's love and spreading his Kingdom.

Meeting the Lord in Imaginative Prayer

The call to friendship with God invites us to allow our lives, with every-thing we most truly are, to become more closely linked to the life, death, and resurrection of the Lord and to everything he truly is. This is what human friendship is about, too, but our friendship with God will take us deep into the hidden treasure within us in a way that no human friendship can fully do. One way to allow this closer linking to happen is to enter imaginatively into scenes from the earthly life of Jesus, in what is called *imaginative meditation*.

Choose a passage that seems to speak to you in some way—a favorite Gospel scene perhaps, or one of the healing miracles. If you don't know which passage to choose, just rest, relax, and ask God to guide you; then wait to see whether any particular scene or event comes to mind. It is important to remember that God isn't waiting for you to chance upon the "right" passage in order to speak to you. He will speak to your heart in some way whatever passage you choose. So be relaxed about it.

When you have chosen a passage, read it several times until it is fa-miliar and you feel at home with it.

Now imagine that the event is happening here and now and that you are an active participant in it. Don't worry if you don't find it easy to imagine it vividly. If you find it difficult to enter into the scene, imag-ine that you are trying to describe it to a child, making it as vivid as pos-sible. And don't worry about getting the facts right. You may well find that your scene doesn't take place in first century Palestine but in Chicago rush-hour traffic, or that the desert tracts of the Good Samaritan story turn into the sidewalks in your neighborhood.

Ask God for what you desire—perhaps to meet him more closely or to feel his touch upon your life.

Fill out the scene as much as you can by, for example, becoming aware of who is there, the surroundings, the sights, the smells, the tastes, the weather, and the feel of the place (peaceful or threatening). What role do you find yourself taking in the scene—for example, are you one of the disciples, a bystander, or the person being healed? Listen inwardly to what God is showing you through your role in the scene.

For example, you may be standing on the edge of the scene and realize that he deeply wants you to come closer so that he can touch your life more powerfully. Or he may be asking you to take seriously a particular call to discipleship that he is suggesting.

Talk with the characters in the scene, especially to Jesus. Speak from your heart simply and honestly. Tell him what you fear, what you hope for, what troubles you. React to him in your prayer as you would react to him if he walked into your room now in bodily form. Don't worry if your attention wanders. If you realize that this is happening, just bring yourself gently back to the scene for as long as you feel drawn to stay there.

There are two absolute rules:

• *Never moralize or judge yourself.*
• *Always respond from your heart and not from your head.*

Neither rule is as easy as it sounds. Many of us carry judgmental attitudes toward ourselves from the past, and we are habitually critical of ourselves. We have also been taught to study the Word of God, and of course it's right to do this. But there is a time, too, for recognizing that our heads can never grasp the truths of God, and that our purpose in prayer is not to defend or condemn ourselves or to come up with any kind of analysis or sermon, but simply to respond, from our inmost depths, to what God is sharing with us of himself.

So allow your feelings and your moods to have their say. If you have feelings of tenderness or apprehension or anger in the situation of your scene, this is telling you something about what is happening between you and God at that particular moment. Just as you take notice of how you are feeling and reacting in your human relationships, so, too, your feelings and reactions in your relationship with God are very significant, even if at times they may appear to be negative. We often learn more from our negative reactions than from the more comfortable ones, just as children learn more from their mistakes than from their perfect scripts.

You may ask—and many people do—how you can be sure that this is prayer and not just a flight of fantasy?

Jesus' words can apply to our prayer: "By their fruit you shall know them." Prayer given by God *always* bears good (though possibly painful) fruit in our lives. Be patient: fruit can take time to grow and ripen.

To answer this question, you may find it helpful to apply these simple tests.

- Has my meeting with the Lord in this way made any difference to my way of being present in the world? Has it opened my eyes in any way, either to my own ways of acting and responding to others, or to the needs and vulnerability of other people around me?
- Is there a sense of consistency between what I feel I have been shown in this prayer and the way I feel the Lord is dealing with me in my life in other ways? If your prayer seems to send you off on a tangent and suggest a decision that is out of line with your personality or your commitments, then it is wise to be cautious. God's ways are usually (but not always!) gentle, and they are reliably consistent.
- Does the prayer leave me feeling basically at peace (even though it may have confronted me with hard challenges), and does the sense of peace continue as time goes on? When we follow our daydreams, the sense of satisfaction is invariably short lived. When the dreams are God's dreams for us, the peace is a lasting one, which will keep recurring and strengthening in our prayer.

You will see that a journey with God in imaginative prayer is a very personal one, unique to every seeker. It can be very helpful to share something of your prayer journey with another human being. This can help you to discern what God is saying to you in your prayer, because as you describe your prayer experience to another person, you will actually be describing it to yourself, and you will often notice threads of meaning then that you might not have noticed during the time of prayer itself. An attentive "tuned-in" listener can reflect back to you what your feelings and responses seem to be and can help you, as it were, to read the compass in your heart that is pointing you toward God.

Focusing Our Inner Lenses

It's probably true that all of us suffer from spiritual double vision. As we noticed in the previous chapter, we live out our lives' actions and decisions, for the most part, from false reference points. How often during the past week have you been conscious of doing something that was truly rooted in your Who center, or of making a decision that was truly taken without fear of loss or hope of gain? How often were you in balance and centered on true north? Sometimes the truth seems light-years away from the tangle of half-truths and compromises, postures, and misleading attitudes in which we find ourselves operating.

However, as we also saw in the last chapter, God is not only our truth but also the way to that truth. The cross is the bridge across the gap between the places where we make our decisions and choose our actions, and the place where we truly are, before God. This bridge spans the expanse of chaos in which we often feel we are operating.

The gospel is the story of the cross, and a map for our personal journey across its bridge, and imaginative meditation is one way of walking across that bridge. When we do so, we are opening our hearts to listen deeply to the Gospel events and stories and asking God to show us our own stories in the Gospel light, to make connections between what we are living vicariously in our prayer and how we are living in our incarnate reality.

Our prayer does one very simple but potentially life-changing thing if we will let it be done to us: it draws these two separate images together and focuses them into a single image, which is God's gift of a personal encounter with his truth for us in the circumstances in which we are actually living and relating to each other.

As this kind of prayer becomes a habit, we become more and more able to connect our lives with the life of the Lord, to find parallels between his teaching and our living. The picture of God-with-us gradually becomes more and more sharp in our hearts, and as it does so, we are empowered to walk forward ever more confidently on our journey as our vision clarifies and deepens and becomes more searching. Clarity of vision brings sureness of step, and terrain that seemed to be wreathed in fog becomes negotiable.

At the same time, choices that are made from false reference points appear ever more obviously out of focus and become disturbing to us. We have made our hearts over to God in prayer, and he is reshaping us and conforming us more and more to his own image, to his own desire for us, and to our own deepest desire for ourselves. When we ask for the grace to see him more clearly, he will answer our prayer, but he will also invite us to see ourselves as we are. This will engender the desire to ask for the grace to conform our lives more closely with the gospel values he is revealing to us.

Learning God's Language

We believe we are the children of God. Children, as I understand it, are born with the innate potential to form every known sound in every human language. Their first attempts at speech are a medley of Babel noise—and indeed, their speech would stay like that were it not for one thing. They all, even the least loved and cared for among them, hear all around them the sounds of one particular human language—their native language. They learn to speak intelligibly (at least to fellow native speakers), first by listening, and then by copying the sounds they hear. Quite simply, they learn the language of those to whom they are closest. A baby whose mother spends time holding her child and talking to it will become articulate more quickly than one who is left alone for most of the day.

The same dynamic seems to apply in the way we learn to express the deepest desires and movements of our hearts. We will express ourselves in the language of the One to whom we are closest. Like a baby, our language will be formed by those we are close to. The further we draw away from God, the more garbled will be our heart's self-expression, until it reverts to the chaos of Babel. The closer we stay to God, the more surely our deeper desires will form around him and his desire for us, and the more our way of being will be conformed to his.

At first our desires crowd around like a baby's first babbling, but slowly our words are forming. We are writing the words of our own personal song of love. It begins in listening and leads to imitation. It draws us, word by word, prayer by prayer, into relationship with the Word, until all our words are superseded and we are ready to be with him in a union of silence.

Staying Close to the Spring

When I think of my own need and desire to stay close to God, I am reminded of a holiday visiting friends in the Czech Republic. We had spent a few days in Prague, where amid blistering heat, the main water supply had failed. No amount of hopeful lingering over the men down the holes outside in the street had brought any enlightenment as to when there might be water again, and our hostess struggled to keep things going as best she could by using the reserve bottles of water she had kept for watering her window boxes. It was two days before things returned to normal.

Soon afterward, we moved on to a remote village in the Bohemian mountains, whose only water supply was a communal spring. It was a joy to pick up the empty buckets and make my way on sandaled feet through the meadow down to the spring. The water bubbled up, full of a life of its own. I would place the bucket under its flow and stand back. No need for more than that. The water did the rest. It took a few minutes for the bucket to fill up, a few minutes of simply watching and waiting. It felt like prayer, simply bringing my empty bucket to the source of life and asking for it to be filled. It was suddenly obvious to me why human beings instinctively make their homes as close as possible to the water supply. And even as I was thinking these thoughts, my prayer seemed to form itself into the words, *"Stay close to the spring."*

These were not reproachful or commanding words, but those of a cherished friend imparting wisdom. Later I asked our host whether the spring ever ran dry. "Only once in living memory," he replied, "and then very briefly." And I remembered the day in Prague when the main supply had failed and left us sweltering and waterless in the burning city heat. All the paraphernalia of main systems and pipes and taps felt like the complications I place between myself and God, and the more complications there are, the more distant I become from him and the more unreliable are my inner resources.

I fell asleep that night with the words from my prayer murmuring through the rafters of the old farmstead: *"Stay close to the spring."* That was several years ago, but the words became an icon for me, to which I often return when my heart is thirsty. You may find, if you explore the experience of imaginative prayer, that your prayer encounters with the Lord will stay with you forever. You can return again and again to this gallery of vivid memories, letting them lead you to ever deeper meanings for your life, until you feel you really do know Jesus as a friend. Yet there will always be mystery in your knowing. He will always take you by surprise. As in any really significant human experience of intimacy, the relationship is not yours to control. Expect to be surprised, and let God do the rest!

To be close to the Lord in his human living, through this kind of prayer, is to be close to the spring. It clears the obstructions and turns our manmade complications into God's own simplicity. It can be trusted, like the spring, and like the spring, it runs pure and free.

Finding God in All Things

There is a marvelous bonus waiting for those who entrust themselves to God in intimate prayer. Just as you bring all your everyday concerns to God in prayer, and talk to him about how you really feel (which may well include expressing your anger and frustration with him from time to time), so, steadily, he will open up more and more of himself to you — or rather, he will increasingly open up your own inner vision, to notice him in everything around you and to recognize his presence in every moment.

I personally have become convinced that there is nothing on earth that doesn't reveal some fragment of the reality of its maker, nor any moment that I live that doesn't hold God concealed within it. Sometimes this is obvious, as in a beautiful sunset. Sometimes it remains hidden.

The Jesuit poet Gerard Manley Hopkins calls it the "inscape" of things —that inner mysterious reality that we might even call their Who center, where God himself is indwelling. People have their inscapes too, and to be in an intimate relationship with someone is to be in touch with their inscape and allow them to be in touch with yours.

We could use the image of a net to help clarify this mystery. When I think of a net in this way, I see a picture of the human family; every knot is a human heart, and every connecting thread is a relationship between those human hearts. And God is indwelling—if we allow him to be—in every heart knot and in every relationship thread. To the extent that he is indwelling, the knot and its connections are sound, and the Holy Spirit flows through the links. To the extent that he is excluded, the net is weakened and torn.

Whenever I attend lovingly to the inscape of another person, I contribute to the strengthening of the net. Whenever I fail to respond to the heart call of another, I weaken the net. It matters how I respond—how I regard my neighbor knots and how I look after the threads that connect us! It matters because this is the net that trawls through the oceans of the world in the hands of the "fishers-of-men." It is the net in which God is gathering his children. Every knot in it has an inscape that is a fragment of God himself, and every connecting relationship is charged with his life and his love. I wish I could say that I always remain aware of this when I am with a difficult person or in a problematic relationship! But the fact that I know what is possible makes it all just that little bit more probable. And I am comforted to remember that the first disciples, too, had to spend much of their time mending nets!

Beyond the Joy

Friendship with the Lord in the intimate relationship of prayer is a gold mine of joy that your explorations will never exhaust.

But friends die. If you have had the experience of walking alongside a dying loved one, you will know that there comes a point when words become meaningless. There is nothing left to say or to do. If you allow the Lord to draw your life into his in prayer, he will sooner or later invite you to walk with him to Calvary.

Like a very close human friend, only much more so, God will settle for nothing less than your absolute truth, the genuine essence of who you really are. He will die for the sake of that truth, and in some form or other he will ask you to join him in that dying and to trust him completely for the freedom and the life to which it is leading.

Friendship, if it connects heart to heart, is always costly. Intimacy with the Lord may cost you all you have. In the next chapter, we will go on to face that cost and that risk, and reflect on what it might mean for the camel of our hearts to pass through the needle's eye of Calvary.

SUGGESTIONS FOR PRAYER AND REFLECTION **13**

I am the true vine,
and my Father is the vinedresser.
Every branch in me that bears no fruit
he cuts away,
and every branch that does bear fruit he prunes
to make it bear even more.
You are pruned already,
by means of the word that I have spoken to you.
Make your home in me, as I make mine in you.
As a branch cannot bear fruit all by itself,
but must remain part of the vine,
neither can you unless you remain in me.
I am the vine,
you are the branches.
Whoever remains in me, with me in him,

bears fruit in plenty;

for cut off from me you can do nothing.

Anyone who does not remain in me

is like a branch that has been thrown away

—he withers;

these branches are collected and thrown on the fire,

and they are burned.

If you remain in me

and my words remain in you,

you may ask what you will

and you shall get it.

It is to the glory of my Father that you should bear much fruit,

and then you will be my disciples.

As the Father has loved me,

so I have loved you.

Remain in my love.

I shall not call you servants any more,

because a servant does not know

his master's business;

I call you friends,

because I have made known to you

everything I have learned from my Father.

You did not choose me,

no, I chose you;

and I commissioned you

to go out and to bear fruit,

fruit that will last.

(John 15:1 – 9, 15 – 16)

TAKE TIME TO BECOME inwardly still, and let these words of Jesus sink you into your heart. Hear him speak them directly and personally to you.

You might like to reflect on how you feel in relation to the vine that holds you in being or in relation to the fruit your life is bearing. We are often as blind to our own fruiting as we are to our sinfulness. Ask God to open your eyes to notice the fruit on your branch of the vine or to see which branches of your life seem barren and which are yielding a harvest.

How do you feel when Jesus calls you "friend"? How do you respond to his invitation to stay close and remain in him?

CHOOSE A FAVORITE Gospel scene or story, and try to imagine yourself a participant in it. As the events unfold, can you identify the two stories that are coming together? One is the Gospel story as it is given to us. The other may be a part of your own personal story that in some way resonates with what you are meeting in the Gospels. Can you see these two pictures side by side? Can you bring them together and let the Lord bring them into a new focus for you? You may feel that there is an unbridgeable gulf between them. If so, tell God so in your prayer, and show him how you are feeling. Or you may find that the Gospel story sheds a new light on this part of your own story. If so, let God lead you more deeply into what he is showing you in this way.

WE ARE URGED to stay close to the spring—that is, close to our innermost center where God dwells. What sacred spaces are there in your life where you feel close to the spring? Which people lead you closer to the spring, and which, if any, tend to lead you further away from it? Look back over the past twenty-four hours. Were there any special moments when you felt particularly close to the spring?

YOU MIGHT LIKE to draw a picture of your own net, showing the knots representing significant people and the threads of relationship that connect you. Reflect prayerfully on the inner mystery, or inscape, of each person and each relationship in your net. Let the specialness of each come into your awareness, and give thanks for it. Are you aware of any holes in your net or any threads that are broken because a relationship is in trouble? Is there anything you can do to mend that bit of your net?

LOOK BACK OVER today, and remember the moments when you have glimpsed the inscape of something or someone — the moment when the hidden reality came alive for you in some way. Remember especially, with gratitude, those times when you have felt that you were relating to someone heart to heart. Have those moments made any difference in how you feel about yourself? About the other person?

 *14*

To Love You More Dearly

W HERE IS GOD in all of this? How often have you asked yourself this question? How often have you been asked the same question by some other distressed soul? How often have we heard it asked out of the middle of some particularly inexplicable news item, reporting the heartrending suffering of the innocent?

And how often have we also heard the standard Christian answer: "God is in the middle of the suffering." And we have assented to that and thought, "Yes, deep down we know that is true." But we have perhaps also wondered what it really means, how it begins to make sense of what we experience, how we could communicate that meaning to others who so badly need to hear it. The question lingers, in spite of our own deeply held faith: Does this answer *really* convince us? Does it make sense of the pain we ourselves feel and the pain we see all around us?"

More than enough books have been written already on the problems of pain and suffering and God's place in it all. The purpose of this chapter is not to add any more to that particular pile of paper. Instead, I invite you to follow a single line of experience that has helped me personally to find God in the anguish as well as in the joy of my living. It lies, I believe, close to the spirit of the Third Week of the *Spiritual Exercises*. This is the line of experience that, quite simply, draws a connection between our personal pain and the agony of Jesus in the last days of his earthly life, so that his pain becomes fused with ours, and ours is taken into his. This may sound like just another pious platitude. Only you can discover whether it has real meaning for your own experience, by letting yourself be drawn into the events of the Passover festival in Jerusalem. . . .

> When we are praying in the spirit of the Third Week, the question is turned around. In response to "Where is God in our experience of suffering and dying?" God challenges us with his own question, "Where are you in mine?"

Connecting to Calvary

In entering into the spirit of the Third Week, we are invited to pray the narrative of Jesus' last days on earth and to discover our own personal connectedness to the events of those days: the Last Supper, the betrayal, the arrest and trial, the torture, death, and burial of God-made-man. The friendship and the intimacy with the living Lord to which the Second Week invited us now brings us up against a moment that we may have experienced in our human relationships, when we are asked to be alongside a loved one who is suffering and dying. To be alongside someone at the very extreme of human experience like this demands our whole truth, the essence of who we really are. There is no more room for platitudes or ambivalence, for flattery or any kind of half-truth.

In Third-Week prayer we are led to discover those places where we are personally present to, and implicated in, the suffering and dying of the Lord. In that discovery, he reveals to our painfully opening eyes the mystery of his own all-powerful presence in ours.

The Cost of Consecration

When we pray with the events of the passion and death of the Lord, we are taking part in a personal Eucharist, in which he is drawing us into the very heart of his own consecration in order to consecrate us for his service. In our prayer, we are consciously connecting the narrative of our own life to the narrative of the Gospels. Our purpose in bringing these two stories together is to allow the power and love of the Lord to become present in our lived experience.

In praying the passion in this way, we come face-to-face with our own involvement in Jesus' experience. For example, we might find ourselves identifying with those who are hammering the nails into Jesus' hands, or betraying him for their own gain, or denying all knowledge of him because of their fears. Or we may want to wash our hands of the whole thing, with Pilate, or run away and hide behind locked doors in the upper room. In other scenes, we may be filled with compassion and taken with the Lord as companions in his captivity and as cosufferers on the cross. Only in the depths of our own prayer will we discover what the passion narrative is making present to our personal lived experience and in what ways it is calling us toward change and transformation. We are, quite simply, bringing Jesus' story into the present tense of our lives.

Recalling the circles of Where, How, and Who from the first chapter, we could say that Third Week prayer brings the reality and the immediacy of God's suffering and death in his Son straight into the heart of our Who center, where it connects to everything we are. It allows us, with real truth, to say, "Your suffering is mine, Lord. In my own small way, I have connected to it and felt it in the secret depths of my prayer. I offer you my heartfelt repentance for my part in causing it, and I offer you my heartfelt compassion in wanting to share it with you and make it a little more bearable."

When we can do this, the transformation begins, and some glimmer of the mystery of redemption starts to penetrate our hearts. We discover that God, there at our center, is responding to us in ways that we might express like this:

> *"Your suffering is mine. Because you have opened yourself up to experience at least a small fragment of my suffering for you, so I shall fulfill my promise and draw you through this experience into the fulfillment of resurrection. The suffering and dying that you experience in your life may not appear to be alleviated in any way, but once your suffering has met mine, the deeper mystery is revealed."*

And what is this "deeper mystery"? Very simple, I think, yet infinitely powerful: *When our suffering is connected in prayer to God's, it becomes, like his, redemptive.*

This is the hidden power and mystery locked up in our suffering and our dying. The act of consecration that our prayer has made possible has released it and made it effective to act upon the givenness of our world and its narratives. It becomes redemptive, not just within the bounds of our own story, but for the story of the suffering of our fellow human beings, and perhaps especially for those we carry personally in our prayer.

Just as we saw in chapter 12, the truth that we encounter in the heart of our sharing of the Lord's passion in our prayer opens up a whole new freedom within us, which in turn becomes the source of an energy that is potentially the very energy of resurrection.

For Breaking and Sharing

For the Eucharist to be fulfilled, the consecrated elements must be broken and shared out in communion. Our consecration means nothing if it is kept to ourselves. Consecration is always for some purpose; it is not an end in itself. A church is consecrated for worship. A pilgrim is consecrated for his or her journey toward God. We are consecrated for God and for each other, not for ourselves alone.

Let's think for a moment about what happens when, for example, we consecrate a church. It seems to me that we do two things:

- We declare our desire and intention that this particular place, this building, shall be a place of worship and a sacred space where God shall be at home.

- We then use that space for the purpose for which it has been consecrated, and in using it, we continue to fulfill the process of its sanctification.

It seems to me that God does the same thing for us when he consecrates us. He declares his desire and intention that we shall be consecrated to his truth and that our lives shall become a space where he can be at home. He then lives in our lives, fulfilling in them the purpose for which he has consecrated them.

Like the Eucharistic bread, we are consecrated in order to be broken and given to others. Like the Eucharistic wine, we are consecrated in order to be poured out for others. Consecration is always a community matter. It is an act of inclusiveness, expressing the all-inclusive love of God.

Consecration, understood in this way, is a vocation for *all* believers, and it has sacrifice at its heart. We can't share in the consecration that was first enacted during the Last Supper and is reenacted in every Eucharist unless we are willing to become part of the sacrifice. Of course, it is easy to say with our lips that we are offering our suffering as part of Christ's sacrifice. And it is easy to believe it in our heads. It becomes a problem when we try to take hold of it in our hearts, because when it reaches our hearts, it takes on a life of its own that rapidly passes beyond our conscious control.

What Does This Mean in Practice?

How might our common human experience of pain connect to Jesus' experience on Calvary? (Note that I say "connect to," not "compare with." There is a huge difference. I can connect to the warmth of the sun, but I am not thereby comparing my own warmth to that of the sun! I can connect my kettle to the main power supply, but I am not comparing its power to that of the national grid!)

Let's look at a few ordinary human stories:

- Colin reported his coworker Frank for moonlighting. He has often regretted it, because Frank was prosecuted for benefit fraud as a result, and his family split up. Colin didn't realize how bad he felt about it until he met himself in prayer in the garden of Gethsemane, planting the traitor's kiss on Jesus' cheek.

- Kate is trapped in the chronic pain of an immobilizing handicap. In prayer she meets herself in the cell where the condemned man, Jesus, spends the night in chains, awaiting trial and execution. She follows him to the cross and shares, in a flow of tears, the stabs of agony as the nails are driven home. She offers her own pain to be joined with his.

- Julie is an appeaser. She will accept any compromise for the sake of avoiding confrontation. When there is trouble, she tries to avoid getting involved, even if others are being hurt. She meets herself in Pilate. Her prayer breaks down in anguish as she finds herself washing her hands of all responsibility for the death of her Lord. She brings her shame to God for healing and forgiveness.

- Mark was violently abused as a child, and now, as an adult, he finds difficulty in controlling his own temper. In prayer he is appalled to find himself lashing out at Jesus with a whip, while some shadowy figure behind him seems to be forcing him to act like this. It is the moment when he comes face-to-face with the full realization of the power his childhood pain still holds over him. It is the turning point toward healing and change.

- Jane's husband, Neil, was crippled in a car crash. Her young life changed overnight from one of unclouded happiness to a journey heavy with the burden of another person's needs and dependency. She often resents it. She finds herself praying, as Jesus did, "Let this cup pass from me." And as she makes the Calvary journey, she meets herself in Simon of Cyrene, who, against his will, is forced to carry Jesus' cross. As she walks on, reluctantly, to Calvary, she comes to realize that the burden she is carrying in Neil is the very means by which God is drawing her into the unimaginable closeness of walking alongside the Lord.

- Richard is a doctor who nursed his own mother through her final struggle against cancer. He sat at her bedside, hour after hour, stroking her head and moistening her lips with a teaspoon of water. After the funeral he suppressed his grief and tried to pick up the threads of his life. Then, in prayer, he finds himself offering the dying Lord a teaspoon of cool water, and as he does so, the grief breaks open in his heart. He watches, aghast, as the soldier pierces Jesus' side, feeling the Lord's pain in his own. And the teaspoon of water he had offered to Jesus as he was dying becomes a healing stream, flowing from Jesus' broken body to bathe not just Richard's own grief but the anguish of all those who will subsequently share their pain with him in years to come.

Piercing the Darkness

These are simple stories of everyday human heartache, stories of the pain we cause each other and the pain we recognize in each other. But they are also pointers toward the possibility of discovering healing, redeeming power in these very places that hurt us most.

When we risk the prayer of Calvary, we are taken to the threshold of a deep darkness. In Gethsemane, Jesus himself struggles "even unto death" with that darkness that we ourselves experience to some extent in our own lives. In the heart of his struggle, he reaches his own point of true north at which he can say, "Thy will be done." When that happens, his pain becomes redemptive. It becomes a shaft of love that is sharp enough to pierce the darkness. The veil of the temple is rent in two, and the glory of the Father is revealed. . . But it doesn't feel like that for us!

Perhaps I might share with you a picture that has stayed with me since childhood and has grown in meaning through the years.

The Star Makers

One of my earliest childhood memories is of a night in winter when I came face-to-face with God while I was walking home from Brownies. If I close my eyes, I can see the place again with as much vividness as it had for me then; I can return to the moment and experience the surge of joy that came coursing through me.

I walked along the darkened side street from the church hall and had almost reached the junction with the brightly lit main road. I can still see the red telephone kiosk on my left and the little sweetshop on my right, with the wasteland beyond it. And it was there, just short of the junction, that something urged me to look up.

The sky came down to meet me and transfixed me there where I stood, for I don't know how many minutes. It seemed like eternity, and perhaps it was. All around me, in every direction, the black night sky was thick with brilliant stars, beckoning me, drawing me closer and closer, utterly eclipsing the streetlights and any lights I had ever seen before. I could have stretched out my child's hands and plucked them down like apples from a tree. The universe was ripe and straining with the load of the silvery harvest, and I stood motionless in its enthralling grip.

As I recall my feelings at that moment, I mostly remember a deep sense of solitude in the face of all this splendor. I was alone in this over-whelmingly lovely eternal space, boundless in its emptiness yet full to overflowing. It was unimaginably vast and distant, yet close enough for me to reach out and touch and hold in my heart. I was quite alone, yet totally unafraid. The stars included space for me and there was nothing to fear.

The memory of that meeting returns to me often. I know now that it was no chance meeting, but one of many over the years that would leave me ever more deeply enfolded in the arms of that loneliness and that splendor, in the arms of the Star Maker.

Many years later, I was taking my first steps into the prayer of the passion and struggling with the disturbing emotions my prayer was bringing into consciousness. There were two moments when my inner eyes came into contact with a darkness that was something much blacker than the darkness of the surrounding night. Yet it was a black-ness not really of threat but, ultimately, of promise, although there was plenty of threat surrounding that seed of promise.

One such moment was in the garden of Gethsemane, when Jesus was led out by the guards and was just passing through a little gate at the edge of the garden. I had a sudden panic at the sight of his depart-ing figure. I called out to him not to leave me there in the garden alone. He turned around in response to my call. He looked straight into my eyes, and as I gazed at his face, I saw in his eyes that deep darkness into which he was allowing himself to be taken. "Come with me," he said, and I followed. The darkness had promise enclosed somewhere inside the threat.

The second moment was on Calvary. I couldn't let him die. I found all kinds of reasons to avoid praying through his death. I couldn't let go. But when the moment was finally reached, I met the deep darkness again. I tried to stretch myself up to the full limits of my height, if only to reach the soles of his feet, but the cross was too high. He was out of my reach. It seemed that at the same moment, he tried to stretch his arms down to me, but they were nailed and rigid, and I was out of his reach. It was the most terrible moment of the prayer, yet also a strangely consoling one, as our eyes met and I again felt him drawing me with him into that darkness that was utterly beyond. We had met in the desolation of not being able to meet, and in that meeting I had clearly heard again that mysterious call into the deep dark.

My life moved on, but these timeless moments of prayer were to return to me again and again, and as I noticed, this happened especially when I met someone who had in some personal way pierced the darkness by embracing their own suffering with a kind of affirmation, as Jesus accepted the chalice of pain in Gethsemane. At such times I find myself standing beneath the stars again, seven or eight years old, but in my heart I carry all the pains and joys of the years between. And every star, every pinpoint of brilliant light, is where someone before me has pierced that darkness, gone through it with trust and with courage, without evasion or circumvention, and broken through, however briefly, to the unimaginable brilliance beyond. And each, in piercing his or her own darkness, has opened up a new source of light, however small and distant, for those of us who still stand trembling in the night.

I am so grateful to those star makers who have gone before, into and through their own inner darknesses. Many of them are personally known to me. Some have gone out of sight forever. Others have touched the brilliance only fleetingly but still carry its fire inside them.

And I know that, in this great company, it might be possible to pass through the little gate of Gethsemane, in whatever forms it may present itself. I know that it will be possible, in some mysterious way, to let my-self be drawn into the deep, dark pools of Jesus' eyes on Calvary and discover the eternal radiance on the other side of darkness. For when every human heart has pierced the darkness, the darkness will be no more, and the Light of the World will be all in all.

An Easy Yoke?

Jesus tells us that his yoke is easy and his burden light. Do you ever shudder when you read that promise, and wonder where you are going wrong, or how Jesus could have so misunderstood your situation? I cer-tainly used to feel like that and tried to suppress the thought and refuse to let my doubts take root.

I think the promise only began to make sense for me when one day in imaginative prayer I found myself in the stable with the newborn Christ and his parents. I wanted to make myself useful, but possibly un-derstanding my inadequacies when it comes to practical talents, Joseph asked me to fetch water from the well to bathe the baby. My prayer took me along the dusty streets of Bethlehem until I reached the well, carry-ing the empty water jar awkwardly in my arms. I filled it up and tried to carry its now nearly unmanageable weight back in the same manner. Of course, the task was impossible. Then a lady came up to me and gently balanced the water jar on my head. She drew my back and shoulders up straight until my body was aligned. Finally, she walked ahead of me slowly, steadily, her whole body finely balanced. I followed her back to the stable without spilling a single drop of water or breaking my back. I even had the peace and the space to enjoy the walk!

On another occasion, I was making my way in rather a labored way up a fairly steep hill in Wales. As I plodded on, four teenage girls came toward me, riding full tilt down the hill on their bikes. As they passed me, every one of them greeted me with a wide, infectious smile, spread-ing their exuberance over me in an overflow of joy. One of them whooped as she rode by. God's own energy, it seemed to me, was pro-pelling them, and gravity was moving them on so effortlessly. They only needed to balance. The rest was pure joy.

When I translate this into the facts of my own lived experience, I discover that balance really does make all the difference. Right at the heart of my own balancing act lies the kind of balance that Jesus teaches us in Gethsemane and on the cross: the balance between our own experience and the truth of God that it is making incarnate, the balance between our own efforts and the still center of ourselves that we discover in prayer, where our true strength lies. When I feel now that my personal burdens are far from light, I try to regain that joy I have known when walking in balance. Of course, it isn't a magic cure for my aches and pains or for the sheer heartache of the Calvary journey, but it touches my truth, and it releases my innermost energies again.

Meeting the Risen Lord

After Jesus' crucifixion, many of his friends encountered his living presence among them. These appearances seemed to be characterized by two features in particular: first, the risen Jesus retained the marks of his agony, and invited his friends to get in touch with the pain in him, as we have done in the earlier part of this chapter. Second, his friends frequently failed to recognize him, at least initially. You might like to take a favorite resurrection scene of your own into your prayer and discover for yourself how the meeting feels for you.

Ignatius suggests that although the Scriptures do not tell us so, Jesus would surely have shown himself to his own mother. Recently, during a retreat, my director suggested that I might spend time in prayer with that imagined scene. At first I was reluctant to do so. My Protestant roots balked at something so nonscriptural. After lunch I set out to walk up the hill and see what the afternoon would bring, with Mary far from uppermost in my thoughts.

The wind was strengthening, but it was a wonderful autumn afternoon. The clouds were banking darkly in the west, but they didn't obliterate the sun that slanted down on the green brown hillside with the glory of furze and the brilliance of berries.

Then, uninvited, Mary was there in my prayer. She was completely alone. She was broken and dumb with grief. She looked back over the thirty years of struggle and doubt, promise and threat, of working to keep the dream alive and grieving to watch it die. Thirty years. For what? Her own grief seemed to come out of her in a long silent howl: Love is dead. . . .

I half expected to see the Lord appear to her, to comfort her and re-assure her of his risen life, but nothing happened. Perhaps I never really believed that it would? She stood there, alone and broken, like an old hawthorn tree, bent against the wind, knowing that even the brief, berry-laden autumn would soon be swept into the mud and lost.

Then there was a sudden change in Mary's mood, as if a new thought had crossed her mind. Her face lifted, and her eyes came to life again; she had noticed me and touched into the pain she was reading in my eyes. She came over to me with a warm wave of compassion. For a moment, her whole desire seemed to be to reach mothering hands into my lonely hurting. Something in me melted and surrendered to her love. Then, just as she reached out her arms and held me to her heart, her gaze was captured by the miracle. I knew that she had met her Son, though he was invisible to me.

"Mary," I whispered. "Is he there?"

"My child," she told me, her voice breathless with joy, "he is stand-ing behind you. You are leaning on him."

I didn't need to turn around. I could feel the power of his holding. But she had met him in her reaching out to me. "Go and do the same," she told me, "and you will meet him, risen and alive, standing always behind those who reach out to you in their need."

I share this personal encounter with you because it seems to say something universal. If we seek the risen Lord, we will find him stand-ing behind each of our brothers and sisters in their need, and he will be-come real for us at precisely the moment when we reach out to them.

Resurrection Now!

The problem with eternity is that it doesn't fit onto our rulers. The infi-nite refuses to be organized into past and future tenses.

> Far from being passive specta-
> tors in the drama of redemp-
> tion, we are cooperating
> participants, whose personal
> God-dream is an essential
> component of the fullness of
> resurrection.

In the Fourth Week of the *Exercises*, we are invited to be present in prayer to the resurrection, and indeed, we may find such experiences in the scenes of Jesus' appearances to his friends. Like all the other Gospel events, these scenes will resonate with something deep in our personal lives if we have ears to hear.

Right at the heart of resurrection is this mysterious sense of the present tense ourselves—the everpresent tense—that is not satisfied by our mere hope of the life to come. In the Fourth Week we confront the paradox of the "now" and the "not yet."

I have my own definition of time, which helps me personally to take hold of this paradox. Time, for me, is only the difference between God's dream and its fulfilling.

I hope that, during our journeying together, I have convinced you of the reality of the Godseed in your heart and directed your attention to the beauty of its growth in you. I feel sure that as soon as a human heart awakens to the life of its Godseed, resurrection begins, not just for that person alone but for the whole human family.

Every time we touch upon our own true north, we touch the resurrection glory. Every time we feel the freedom that flows when we are living true, we are feeling the flow of eternity. Resurrection is a now moment, a sacramental moment that at once both points toward and brings about the fulfilling of God's dream. It is the working out, in time, of God's eternal dream, and each of us is engaged in it in every breath we take.

SUGGESTIONS FOR PRAYER AND REFLECTION 14

Then Jesus came with them to a small estate called Gethsemane; and he said to his disciples, "Stay here while I go over there to pray." He took Peter and the two sons of Zebedee with him. And sadness came over him, and great distress. Then he said to them, "My soul is sorrowful to the point of death. Wait here and keep awake with me."

(Matthew 26:36–38)

TRY TO IMAGINE yourself present as Jesus leaves the Last Supper and makes his way to Gethsemane. How do you feel? What do you do?

When you arrive at the garden, Jesus draws aside into the shadows to pray. He asks one or two friends to go with him. Where are you in the scene now?

Hear his words, out of the darkness: "Stay with me. . . . Keep watch with me. . . ." How do you feel when you hear these words? How do you respond?

CAN YOU REMEMBER any moments in your journey with God when you felt that you were being consecrated by him for a particular ministry or role in life? You may perhaps remember your confirmation, or a time of spiritual renewal, or the growing awareness of a vocation; or the moments may have been very private, in times of prayer. Recall them now, before God. If you feel drawn to do so, perhaps renew the promises you made to God at those times, and ask him to bless your continuing intention to follow him in those special ways.

DO YOU KNOW any star makers? These would be any people who have known a deep darkness in their lives, perhaps through pain or handicap, abuse or cruelty, loneliness or depression, and have in some way pierced the darkness, taking their personal pain through a spiritual barrier and becoming a source of strength, encouragement, or enlightenment for others. Give thanks to God for them now. If you feel it is possible or appropriate, you might like to find a way of letting them know how much you honor their courage.

WHAT BURDENS do you feel you are carrying in your life today that seem almost too heavy to bear? Name them to God in your prayer, and tell him honestly how you feel. Then try to bring your inner compass to stillness, and ask God to hold your heart in the perfect balance of true north. While you are at that still center of peace, take up the burden again, and ask God to balance it across your shoulders in his way.

WHERE IS THE worst area of pain in your life at present? Let it come into your awareness in prayer. Lay every feeling before God without fear. This is your Gethsemane. Ask the Lord to stay with you and to watch and pray with you. Ask him to draw your pain into his own. Read and pray through any of the Gospel accounts of Jesus' suffering, his trial, his torture, and his death. In what parts do you feel closest to him? Why do you think this is? How is his experience connecting to your own?

MAKE A CONSCIOUS attempt to still yourself when another person is standing in front of you, and remember that the risen Lord is standing right behind that person. Would that make a difference to your way of relating to them? Repeat the exercise whenever you have a chance, until it starts to become a habit. Try it especially when someone is being difficult, is making demands on you, or is in need of your love in some particular way.

15 ◎

To Follow You More Nearly

THE *SPIRITUAL EXERCISES* end with a contemplation that invites us to reflect on how we will respond to the immense love that God has shown to us, and with a prayer of personal surrender of the gift of our hearts and lives to the One who holds us in his own heart. We have begun to see him more clearly and to see our own lives in his gospel light. We have asked to love him more dearly—enough to walk with him into his passion and death and, beyond that, to resurrection. Now that seeing, that loving, inspire in us the desire to follow him more nearly. How will you make that "following" a reality in your life?

Of course, your response to this question is a matter for your heart alone. In this chapter, I would like to share a few of the challenges that have arisen from my own reflections about how it might be possible to begin to respond to God's gift of unconditional love.

Let me begin by introducing you to two friends of mine; let us call them Marjorie and Frank. Marjorie is a social worker who went into that kind of work later in life. As a younger woman, she brought up two children of her own and two adopted children. These last two were both from deeply disturbed backgrounds, and Marjorie and her husband, Frank, have given years and years of their lives to sheltering, nurturing, and guiding these two seriously damaged young lives.

When she lost her job as a laboratory assistant through downsizing, Marjorie went back to college, taking her life experience with her in the hope that she might be able to make it fruitful for other people. She has

179

finished her studies now and is working day by day with troubled families and with those who are themselves adopting distressed children. This work often takes her into the courts, where she is sometimes called upon to give evidence as an expert witness.

Expert evidence! Most of us would not see ourselves as likely to be called to be expert witnesses in a court of law. Yet listen to what St. Paul has to say:

> *Life to me is not a thing to waste words on, provided that when I finish my race I have carried out the mission the Lord Jesus gave me—and that was to bear witness to the Good News of God's grace.*
>
> (Acts 20:24)

We all know that we are called to witness to our faith and for our God. Most of us have, perhaps, a rather vague notion of what that might mean, and none of us can ever know in advance what it might cost. Marjorie's story may help a little. Being a witness means giving evidence. It means having that particular quality that reveals something of God to those around us. It means that the Godseed in our hearts has germinated and is showing some outward sign of life—in growth, in blossom, or in fruit. If our lives reveal no evidence of the God indwelling our hearts, then we are of no use as witnesses.

So what might it mean to be called as expert witnesses, as Marjorie is sometimes called upon to do?

The word *expert* is related to several other words in our language. It is the past participle of a verb that means "to experience." An expert is one who has experienced. It comes from the Latin verb *experior,* which means "to try, prove, test, undertake, attempt, risk, undergo, experience, contend with."

Of all these shades of meaning, perhaps the most telling for our spiritual journey is "to risk." When we take the risk of faith, we open ourselves up to the *experience* of God, and that experience is our proof, living and lived proof, of his reality and his power and his love—proof first to ourselves and then to others who begin to notice its effects on us.

Expert has the same root as the word *experiment*. An expert is one who has experimented, one who has tried things out to test their truth and their reality.

And now, here in the last chapter of these explorations in Ignatian spirituality, is it not true to say that this is what we have been doing—not just in our sharing of these pages but in our individual lives and faith journeys over the years? We have been risking the exposure of our innermost being to God in prayer, and reflecting on that experience, and testing the truth of our own discernment in the light of how it affects our real daily lives.

If we look back now to the question "What can I give him?" we can perhaps approach the answer in two ways. First, there is an answer that applies to all of us, and in which we can share and help each other. Second, there is an answer that applies to each of us individually and can be fully known only between each of us and God.

We could summarize these two answers like this:

- *I am called to be an expert witness for Christ in the court of his creation.*
- *I am called to become fully who I most truly and eternally AM.*

So what can I give him . . . ?

- *I can give him the evidence of my lived experience as a sign of his real and loving presence in the world.*
- *I can give him back—fulfilled—the dream he first had of me when he created me.*

The first is a collective gift to God. The second is an individual gift that each of us must work out for ourselves with God, in our prayer and in our living.

Giving Expert Evidence

What makes a witness into an expert witness? Witnessing to God can be done just with words, from the head, but *expert* witnesses reveal God out of their lived experience of him and in the authority of his truth that they hold in their hearts.

The Latin expression *experto crede* means "You can take my word for it because I have tried." Can we apply this expression to our own belief in the reality of God in our lives and our world? As we consider this thought, it might be helpful to break it down into stages. Reflect for a few minutes on these more personal questions:

- Have I actually tried (experimented)? Have I tried walking with God through the ordinary events of my ordinary days? Have I tried noticing each night, where, when, and in whom I have especially sensed his presence? Have I tried tracking my own moods and noting when I felt close to God and when I felt far away? Have I tried listening to him, at a personal level, in my prayer and in his word, and letting what I hear take root in how I live?

- If I have tried it, do I trust my own experience of God? When I feel him leading me in a particular direction, do I trust his reality sufficiently to risk following him? Remember the story of the man who entertained the crowds by pushing a wheelbarrow across a tightrope drawn across a gaping chasm. "Do you believe I can do it?" he asked them. "Of course we do," they shouted. "Who will get in the wheelbarrow, then?" he invited. And they all fell silent. Do I merely believe that God holds my life in his hands, or do I trust his guiding in my living of it?

- If I trust my own experience of God, do I have the courage to stand up and show that trust, even when that means swimming against the flow? Standing up to be counted doesn't, I feel, primarily mean standing up and proclaiming our faith in words to reluctant bystanders (though it might). Marjorie and Frank, for example, are committed Christians, and they know that Christ is the source of all the power and love in their lives, but they don't tell people this unless they are asked. There is no need. It would be like giving a botany lecture while standing under a cherry tree in the full glory of its blossoms beneath a blue May sky. The reality is so much more eloquent and potent than the mere scientific facts. Marjorie's and Frank's lives blossom and bear fruit with the life of their Lord, and that is what gives such force and authority to their expert evidence.

There are three questions to consider:
Have I tried it?
Do I trust it?
Will I let it show?

Giving Back the Dream

We began this journey of exploration by reflecting on who we most truly *are* at the heart of ourselves, where the Godseed is planted. It is here in the Who center that God's dream for us is unfolding. Our lives are the space in which that dream takes shape, and our gift to our God is his dream fulfilled.

We have seen something of what it might mean to become cocreators in God's dream for us. We have seen how we first need to recognize that heart of ourselves where God is, incarnate in each of us as he was incarnate in his Son, who called us his brothers and sisters. We have also observed that we are free to direct our lives either home toward our God center or out and away from it. Then come the fears and false images of God, the addictions and attachments that obstruct the unfolding of our dreams and divert energy from realizing our deepest desires.

God's dream in our hearts is a tender but all-powerful seed. We are charged with the task of bringing the dream to birth. How can we do that? Ignatius suggests a way that leads, through prayer, to an ever deepening intimacy with the Lord in his earthly ministry, in his passion, and in his resurrected life. Day by day, prayer by prayer, lived moment by lived moment, we notice and respond to the constant encounters with the living God, and every time we do so, our roots are strengthened, and the Godseed grows a little closer toward becoming a unique manifestation of its Creator.

There is no great mystery surrounding this process—it can all be expressed very simply. Our increasing intimacy with God will inevitably foster the desire in us to become the person he is dreaming us to be. When that is our deepest desire, that will be what eternally *is*. By surrendering the lesser desires of our lives and submitting to whatever kinds of dying that entails, we will cross the threshold of resurrection, just as he promised we would.

Toward the end of his *Exercises,* Ignatius invites us to reflect again on all the ways in which God has revealed his overflowing love to us, personally and in community. We are being drawn, through our own deepest desires, back into the perfect love union that is expressed by the Trinity. In a very real way, this is the center of our being, to which our inner journey is destined.

We began by reflecting on our journey to the truest heart of ourselves, where God is indwelling, and then out again, carrying the transforming treasure from the center to the outermost edges of our lives. Now we can see this movement on a much larger scale, as a journey into the heart of the Trinity, where each Person is in perfect interrelationship with, and is interdependent on, the others.

This relationship is the circle of eternal joy in which God so rejoices that he calls us to share it eternally with him, because the Trinity is the divine model for human community. He asks us and empowers us to carry the transforming experience back to our still untransformed world until our human community becomes his Kingdom.

Carrying God in a Bottomless Bucket

Carrying God to the world sounds like a tall order—and if we think we really can do that, we may be teetering on the brink of a Messiah complex.

There was a time when I used to think that we could receive grace from God into our own containers, rather like the old days when people used to take their jugs and jars out to the milk cart to get their daily supply of milk. How much you got depended on the size of your container. When it came to grace, I thought, I would receive as much as my heart would hold, and if I hoped for more, I would have to do something about expanding my heart. This way of looking at things served me reasonably well for a while (even though, as you can see, it is rather a me-centered approach to the problem)—until the bottom fell out of my bucket.

Maybe there have been times in your life when your system gave out and your tried-and-tested methods of doing things just didn't seem to work anymore. Maybe it was some traumatic experience that brought you to a fuller realization of your own inability to save even yourself, let alone the rest of the world. Or maybe it was just the gradual advance of a sense of personal helplessness when it came to questions arising out of your journey with God. Whatever it was, it quite possibly left you feeling as though your certainties had become unreliable and the jug you had been using to collect your "daily grace" from the milk float of your prayer had sprung a leak.

Every life is shot through with little deaths. At the time, they seem only to diminish us, but over time, if we look back reflectively, they may reveal themselves as the very moments when we really came alive. The bucket becomes a pipe. The few liters of grace we might have held in our bucket turn into the possibility of a constant stream that—at last— is free to flow through our open-ended hearts.

We can no longer bracket ourselves with neat beginnings and end- ings, and when God removes our brackets and leaves us feeling naked and bereft, he is actually throwing open our limiting barriers and ex- posing us to the pain and the glory of eternity. We experience pain be- cause we cannot bear lightly the truth that we are not the purpose of it all, but only the provisional containers through which the Purpose flows; and glory, because that Purpose is so infinitely greater than any- thing our blinded hearts could ever have imagined.

Once the ends are off our life's pipeline, and the certainties we thought we held are dissolved in the acid of experience, grace can flow freely. Or not so freely? For myself, honesty demands that I acknowledge the many blockages and resistances that cling to the walls of my own heart's channel like limpets to a boat's hull. Detaching the limpets is painful. Yet even here, there is great promise: the more freely grace flows, the more clear the channel becomes. What began as the merest trickle will swell, and the more power it gathers, the more surely it will remove my barnacles.

> It seems to me to matter very much how we choose, because in every moment we are either condemning the world and ourselves to a little bit more of death or releasing them to a little bit more of life.

I cannot give God to the world. Only God himself can do that. But I *can* give him some space, and if space is what I seek, where might I find it if not in my own inner emptiness—in those places that hurt me so much that I try to fill them up with achievements and attachments? When I learn to let go of those false friends, then space is something I find I have plenty of. I can give God my empty, broken bucket to be a little segment in a channel for his peace.

Catacombs or Honeycombs?

We all know the story about the two men who looked out from prison bars, and one saw mud, the other stars. It can sound all so easy, and we know, too well, that the stars are not always in evidence. Some of the explorations in this book have underlined the possibilities of reflecting on our own experience, day by day, to discover where God has been in them—to discover, as it were, the golden threads of meaning, truth, and joy that run through our days. We have also become aware of the extent to which we decide our own destinies by choosing how to respond to the givenness of our lives. In terms of the circles, we respond to our circumstances in the How circle, and how we respond makes us see the Where in new ways. These new ways, in turn, gradually shape and transform our Who.

Suppose we were left—as well we may be, on the other side of death's mystery, with only our Who to bring home to God. What would it look like? When we come into the fullness of God's presence, what will we be holding in our hands? A honeycomb or a catacomb?

Whichever it is, it will have been formed out of the many cells of our every days. Every time we look out of the prison bars and see the mud; every time we fall asleep recalling only the irritations and problems of the day; every time we look into the face of our neighbor and see the faults, we have sealed another grave chamber for the death of our Godseed. Every time we look out from our constraints and shackles and see a star; every time we look back over a day and see a moment's joy; every time we look into our neighbor's eyes and see the love inside him, we open up a cell of sweetness for the delight of our own hearts and the world's.

The bees create honeycombs unconsciously in the course of simply fulfilling their own deepest desire. We might, in our prayer, ask God for the grace to do likewise.

Knitting Squares for the Kingdom Blanket

When I was little, ham-fisted, and left-handed (now I am large, ham-fisted, and left-handed), my aunt used to try, very patiently, to teach me to knit. Eventually, after a gigantic struggle, I learned to knit my way across the rows and even managed to produce a few knitted squares to contribute to the refugee blankets we used to make in those days. But I always needed my aunt's help to cast on and cast off. Those operations remained mysteries beyond my comprehension.

All this arose for me again one day in prayer, and I could see the stitches in my square as a sort of parable of the events and relationships in my life. Every stitch was an essential and unique part of the fabric of my square. God cast me on to the needles of my own particular circumstances when I was conceived, and gradually, painstakingly, I have learned to form my stitches. Sometimes I got them wrong—too tight or too loose; sometimes I dropped them completely and had to live with the hole. Sometimes I tore into the wool with my needles and made myself—or others—bleed. Sometimes I glowed with pride as a row was successfully completed. Sometimes I wept with frustration. Sometimes I wanted to tear the whole thing apart and start again, with different wool, on different needles.

I'm still knitting . . . but I have a friend who is dying. As he makes the longest journey, from life to Life, he is surrounded by his memories. His room is graced, really graced, with rows of fine stitches: photographs of people who have been significant to him, poems and meditations, icons and gifts he has treasured, music that has inspired him, the books he has written, the children he has fathered, the wife he has loved. He has substantial memories, and dreams worth keeping.

His wool is almost worked. Soon he will be bringing the square of his life to God. In these months I have had the unimaginable privilege of standing alongside as he and God have been casting off. . . .

One by one he surrenders his stitches. The process is bittersweet, shot through with pangs of grief and heartbreak, yet transfigured by the promise of what is being completed.

I know that soon he will hear the words of heaven: *Consummatum est.* "It is completed. The square I gave you to knit is finished." Perhaps he asks himself, as I do when I look to my own casting off, "Will the Lord accept the square I bring him for the Kingdom blanket?"

And I think then, that it isn't going to matter so much about the mistakes and the spoiled patterns and the dropped stitches. What is going to matter is the one crucial question: "Does it help to keep my people warm?" Which will be valued more: a blanket full of faults and holes, to keep them warm, or the perfect masterpiece that you never made?

MY FRIEND TELLS me that now, when he passes the shelf of books that he has written, they seem to whisper to him, "Now, live what you have written." I pass those whispered words on to you. "Now, let us live what we have discovered."

A Prayer of Surrender

Ignatius made this his prayer of surrender. It is not a prayer to be made lightly. God may answer it in ways you do not expect.

Take, Lord, and receive
my liberty,
my memory,
my understanding,
my entire will,
everything I have and call my own.

You gave me all these gifts,
and to you I return them.
Dispose of them entirely according to your will.
Give me only your love and your grace.
That is all I ask.

Here is my personal interpretation. It is inspired by Hannah's surrender of her longed-for child, Samuel. Her deepest desire has been fulfilled in Samuel's birth, and she responds by recognizing her even deeper desire to offer what she most cherishes to the Lord. She gives Samuel to the Lord. You might like to reflect on how your own deep desires are being fulfilled and how far you feel able to surrender the treasure of your heart into the hands and the authority of God. Use this prayer if it helps you, or perhaps you would like to formulate your own.

Take and Receive

"This is the child I prayed for, and Yahweh granted me what I asked him.
Now I make him over to Yahweh for the whole of his life.
He is made over to Yahweh."

There she left him, for Yahweh. (1 Samuel 1:27–28)

I place myself into your hands, Lord.
Take me and receive me.
Take me, for I am yours.
Receive me, for I give myself freely to you.

I place my liberty into your hands.
It sets me free to love and to serve. It gives me the great gifts of choice and self-determination. But it tempts me into choosing the lesser good, the lesser gods. It leaves me free to choose for myself, instead of for love. It beguiles me into believing only in myself. It allows me to choose to do harm, to destroy, and to die.
Take, receive my liberty under your leadership.
It is made over to the Lord.

I place my memory into your hands.

It draws me back to times and places past where I have known your touch upon my life. It leads me through my history to your mystery. But it holds in its power all my "if onlys." It tangles its brambles around my heart, fixing me in past hurts and harms, causing me to look back and turn to salt, corrosive with resentment. It holds me unforgiven in past wrongs that you have healed. It darkens my hopes with regrets.

Take, receive my memory under your leadership.

It is made over to the Lord.

I place my understanding into your hands.

It leads me more deeply into your Truth, but it binds me in the narrow spaces of my own little truths. It gives me insight to help me understand the way others respond to life. It gives me the words and the structures to express my own responses. But it tempts me into settling for human understanding when you are calling my soul toward the divine. It lures me into the cul-de-sac of pride and self-satisfaction when I want to be satisfied with nothing less than you.

Take, receive my understanding under your leadership.

It is made over to the Lord.

I place my imagination into your hands.

It carries me to the heavens, as fireworks burst across the night sky. It leads me into heart knowledge, spanning time and space to make all things present. It kindles the flame of your truth in the darkness of my own mind. But it also feeds my fears. It seduces truth into fantasy and caution into dread. It opens up the gateway to your reality, or it traps me in the self-imposed enclosures of my own make-believe.

Take, receive my imagination under your leadership.

It is made over to the Lord.

I place my power to feel into your hands.

My feelings draw me into the depth and joy of love. They invite my life stream to pour into yours. They open my arms and my heart and unlock my griefs and my longings. They also suck me down the spirals

of bitterness and despair and hold me captive to my passing moods.
They are a candle, warm with love light, or the destructive sweep of a
forest fire.

Take, receive my feelings under your leadership.
They are made over to the Lord.

I place my entire will into your hands.
Once, when time began, it was in harmony with yours. But sin
fragmented your creation, and every creature took hold of its own little
world and ruled according to its own narrow will. I want it to be otherwise, but my wanting achieves nothing because my will remains stubbornly my own.

Take, receive my entire will under your leadership.
It is made over to the Lord.

Give me only your love and your grace, for that is all I need.
Then I, too, shall be made over to the Lord.

SUGGESTIONS FOR PRAYER AND REFLECTION 15

Six days before the Passover, Jesus went to Bethany, where Lazarus was, whom he
had raised from the dead. They gave a dinner for him there; Martha waited on
them and Lazarus was among those at table. Mary brought in a pound of very
costly ointment, pure nard, and with it anointed the feet of Jesus, wiping them with
her hair; the house was full of the scent of the ointment. (John 12:1–3)

IMAGINE THAT YOU are in the house of Mary, Martha, and Lazarus when
Jesus arrives to spend the evening with you. The brother and two sisters
are all present to Jesus in quite different ways in this story, each according to his or her personality. How will you respond to the Lord during
this meeting? What will be your particular way of showing your love for
him? In your prayer, let yourself respond to him in whatever way you

feel drawn to do. How does he react to your gift of love? How do you feel about the gifts that others are giving him? How do you feel as you make your gift to him? Speak to him, and tell him your feelings. Listen to him as he tells you his.

Suppose you were asked to be an expert witness to the reality of God in your own life. What parts of your lived experience do you feel especially reveal the power and love of God to yourself and to others? In which areas of your life do you feel able to say to others, "God is real; God is love; God is power. You can take my word for it because I have tried."

When you give God the dream that your life has grown, out of his Godseed in your heart, how do you think you might describe that unique fulfillment that is yours, and yours alone, to discover? What characteristics will it have? What will be its special beauties and properties? What is God growing in your heart, even now, that is going to be a dream worth keeping? Don't be shy about your God dream. You are only giving back to God the fulfillment of what he has first given to you. You are giving him of his own. Give it joyfully, without false modesty.

Have there been any times when the bottom has fallen out of your bucket? With hindsight, can you see that any of those times have become times of grace? If so, give thanks to God for them in your prayer, and ask him to turn your trickle into his abundant flow.

Where are the empty spaces in your heart? Is there loneliness, disappointment, heartache, grief? Do you feel able to make that emptiness over to God, as a space for him to fill with grace for you and for others? Are you aware of any blockages in your channels caused by things with which you have tried to fill up your emptiness?

Reflect back over the past twenty-four hours. Every minute has potentially contributed to death or to life—building a catacomb or a honeycomb. Which parts of today have been contributing to the burial of your Godseed; and which have been helping to bring it to life and growth?

IMAGINE YOUR LIFE as a knitted square. Can you see the parts where you dropped your stitches and lost your pattern? Now feel the warmth of the wool between your fingers. Which do you think is more important to the refugee who will use your blanket—its accuracy or its warmth? Let yourself cherish each stitch as a unique event or relationship in your life. Value it, and thank God for it as it is, not for what it might have been.

REFLECT ON THE Prayer of Surrender on pages 188–189. If you feel drawn to do so, write your own version of it, bringing to God the gifts of your being and asking him to receive them into his authority, for he is indeed their Author and their Source.

BENEDICTUS

WE BEGAN this journey by smiling over Wainwright's instruction to turn left at the third hawthorn tree. It was a landmark pregnant with invitation. This was fine if you were standing at the beginning of the path, map in hand, ready to notice all the right landmarks and make all the best possible turnings to lead you home to your deepest desire. . . .

But most of us don't start the journey at the beginning, or even at any other sensible prescribed point. We begin, quite simply, from where we are, and for most of us that will be long after we have already missed the third hawthorn tree and perhaps a good few other apparently vital landmarks. I am reminded of the traveler who lost his way and asked for directions. After a long and convoluted explanation of how to reach his destination, his informant gave up, with the comment, "But if I were you, I wouldn't start from here."

God knows better. With God we always start exactly where we are, and he is both the path and the compass. So it becomes possible to stop for a moment on the journey and look back at the maze of paths behind us. Like most of you, perhaps, I can now see several hawthorn trees where I took the wrong turn. In Ignatius's language, I made the wrong "election." So what can I do about it now? Stand and regret? Or go back to the bottom of the hill and try again? Or remember that God is Now

and God is Here, wherever we are, in whatever unchosen places or situations, and that
it is God whom we seek, not a particular
path.

God, being who he is, gives his special blessing upon those very places
where we ourselves feel most vulnerable, broken, and lost.

I remember at school singing the hymn
"God is working his purpose out, as year
succeeds to year." At the time, I suspected that this was wishful thinking or that, if it were true, this purpose would always be a mystery to
me. I know better now. I know that my own deepest desires are gradually drawing me closer to God's desire for me. I can look back now over
a fair length of my own path and see some of the other paths I might
have taken. Some of them may seem (from here) to have offered an easier, more direct route home, but I can never, shall never, need never
know what pitfalls they might have been concealing. All I need to know
is that wherever I am is where I am with God, in the here and now, and
that this journey, which is my real vocation, is unfolding itself out of all
my life's choices—wise and unwise—as a skilled weaver might create
his cloth out of all kinds of unlikely bits of wool.

Let us share God's blessing now, free of regret for the landmarks we
have missed, alert and alive with trust for all that lies ahead. . . .

*I bless the poverty in your heart, which knows its own emptiness, because
that gives me space to grow my Kingdom there.*

*I bless that in you that touches others gently, because everyone responds to
gentleness, and gentleness can capture even hardened hearts.*

*I bless that in you that grieves and aches for all that is lost or can never be,
because that is my opportunity to comfort you with my much greater love.*

*I bless that in you that longs and strives after your own deepest truth and
after truth for the world, because even as you pray, I am constantly satisfying
these deep unspoken longings.*

*I bless you every time you show mercy and forgiveness, because that is like
a little window in your heart, setting you free from resentment and opening up
a space for me to enter and to heal.*

*I bless the purity of your heart, because that is the elusive center where your
deepest desire meets mine. That is where we meet face-to-face.*

I bless the peacemaker in you, that in you that seeks the peace that passes understanding, knowing the cost of its obtaining, because that is what I sent my Son to give, and in your peace making you become my daughter or son.

I bless even those things in your experience of journeying with me that feel like persecution and abuse and misunderstanding, because they are the proof that your faith is no illusion.

These, Lord, surely, are your original blessings, that precede and supersede my original sin and assure me that your joy, your peace, and your love are so much larger than my fearing and my failing. Yes, this is the gospel of the Lord.

Where you are (however unchosen) is the place of blessing.
How you are (however broken) is the place of grace.
Who you are, in your becoming, is your place in the Kingdom.